FRANK SERAFINI

Interactive
Comprehension
Strategies

Fostering Meaningful Talk About Text

 SCHOLASTIC

New York • Toronto • London • Auckland • Sydney
Mexico City • New Delhi • Hong Kong • Buenos Aires

Scholastic Inc. grants teachers permission to photocopy material in the appendices for personal classroom use.
No other part of this publication may be reproduced in whole or in part or stored in a retrieval system, or transmitted in any
form or by any means, electronic, mechanical, photocopying, recording, or otherwise, without written permission of
the publishers. For information regarding permission, write to Scholastic, 524 Broadway, New York, NY 10012.

Editor: Lois Bridges

Production management: Amy Rowe

Cover design: Maria Lilja

Interior design: Sydney Wright

Copy editor: Jennifer DePrima

ISBN-13: 978-0-545-08318-8
ISBN-10: 0-545-08318-4
Copyright © 2009 by Frank Serafini

Contents

Acknowledgments

I would like to thank Sophie Ladd for all of her help during our research on classroom talk. You are a great doctoral candidate! I would also like to thank some of my favorite authors and illustrators of picturebooks, Maurice Sendak, David Weisner, and Anthony Browne for creating such masterpieces of literature. These artists are the reason children love to read.

Introduction

> The primary goal of the reading workshop is to expand and enhance the way that students and teachers think and talk about the written texts and visual images they encounter throughout their lives.
>
> —*Frank Serafini*

The title of this book, *Interactive Comprehension Strategies: Fostering Meaningful Talk About Text*, brings together two separate yet intimately connected concepts: talk and comprehension. The better we comprehend what we are reading, the more effectively we can talk about the text, and as we talk about the text, we extend and refine our comprehension. Clearly, it's a win-win—talking and comprehending go hand in hand. Let me discuss talk and comprehension separately before I address them together.

To begin, *talk* is ubiquitous. Everyone does it, especially classroom teachers. However, we rarely talk about talk. Why? After all, talk shapes every move we make in our classrooms, and the talk we use, especially during our reading lessons and literature discussions, is pivotal. Through talk, most concepts are absorbed, most information is shared, and our own ideas are negotiated and reconsidered. So why isn't talk a bigger subject in educational circles? If classroom teachers aren't talking about talk, they should be, and I hope this book draws their attention to this essential aspect of literacy instruction.

We demonstrate what we know through talking and we learn new things by listening to others talk. What could be more basic to literacy education? Yet a preponderance of the educational publications that focus on reading instruction, even ones I have written myself, tend to focus on the objectives, procedures, and resources used for effective comprehension lessons, rather than on the language used to enact those lessons. Indeed, I believe that the ways teachers talk with their students have more effect on the quality of actual lessons than the resources teachers select or the procedures they set in place.

James Britton (1970) once stated, "Talk is the ocean on which all learning floats." What an insightful commentary! If this is true, then talk is also the medium that keeps teaching afloat. Without talk, teaching—particularly teaching someone to comprehend—is a very difficult proposition. Because of this, this book focuses on the language teachers use to enact quality reading lessons and literature discussions. In other words, we need to examine and investigate the language we use to keep our literacy instruction afloat.

Now, let's consider the second term, *comprehension*. This is a bit more complicated. Comprehension has to do with knowing, what can be known, and how we come to know. It's about meaning. It's about what counts as knowledge and how we demonstrate to others that we understand something. One of the primary ways we demonstrate that we know something in school is by being able to talk or write about it. Doctoral programs require students to complete written dissertations and participate in oral exams to demonstrate that they have understood the required content of their field. Students write essays in school to demonstrate they have read the required materials and have achieved a basic understanding of the concepts presented. Does talking and writing about what you have read provide enough evidence to claim comprehension?

Our challenge is to avoid reducing comprehension to literal details and recall. Reducing comprehension to literal recall affects the kinds of talk that occur in the classroom, the questions teachers ask, and the answers they expect students to give.

In other words, our definition of comprehension affects the ways we speak with and respond to students. It's a waste of time to talk about talk without also addressing what we should be talking about. If we want our literature discussions to be more sophisticated, more engaging, and more analytical, we have to expand what we allow and support in our discussions.

Maybe a quick example would be beneficial here. If we think that comprehension is about literal facts and details contained in a text, the questions we ask and the discussions we conduct tend to focus on these literal details. We ask questions that students must answer by drawing directly from textual references. However, if we think that real comprehension has to do with inferring ideas about the world from the text, or questioning what is written, or challenging the author's intentions and assertions, we are drawn to discuss texts in deeper and novel ways. Clearly, the way we think about texts affects how we talk about texts. In addition, if we listen to what students are sharing and we have some faith that what they say is worth considering, then the way we talk about texts may influence the ways in which we think about them. The discussions we conduct are directly influenced by our definition of comprehension, and our definition of comprehension is influenced by the content of our discussions.

How Talk Frames Our Comprehension of Text

I wonder: what comes first—a change in the way we talk, or a change in the way we think? I have come to the conclusion that the answer is neither; rather, both work together to influence each other. The way we talk and the conversation we hear in response change the way we think, and the way we think changes how we talk.

This book addresses the following ideas:

♦ *Traditional interaction patterns.* We begin by striving to understand traditional ways of discussing books in schools. This "institutionalized" way of talking has a profound effect on what teachers are led to believe is appropriate instruction.

♦ *Language of instruction versus language of discussion.* Our instructional interactions and teaching language are not the same. We must understand and address these differences if we are going to be more effective in both instructional contexts.

♦ *Expectations for discussions.* The expectations we set in the classroom for how we want students to talk with one another and the content of these discussions set the tone for the discussions that become possible. Students need clear, attainable expectations that support the discussions we know are most productive.

♦ *Types of questions.* The kinds of questions teachers ask, the number of questions they ask, and the types of responses they accept and "sanction" are pivotal considerations for comprehension instruction.

♦ *Strategies for interactive discussions.* The goal of literature discussions is to enhance the understandings and abilities of all students involved. The more sophisticated, engaging, and interactive the discussions, the better they support students' abilities to analyze, comprehend, and reconsider what they read.

♦ *Readers' interpretive repertoires.* To help our students become more sophisticated readers, we need to provide them with interpretive repertoires, ways of approaching and analyzing what they read.

My "Road to Talk"

I began my academic publishing career in 2001 with the publication of *The Reading Workshop: Creating Space for Readers* (Serafini, 2001). This book focused on my "big picture" of reading instruction. Throughout the book, I described how I organized my classroom, my daily schedule of events, and the various components of my reading workshop such as read-alouds, comprehension strategy instruction, and literature study groups. I tried to provide classroom teachers with a framework to support new approaches to reading and literacy instruction. For the next several years I continued to speak and write about the reading workshop and its components. In 2004 I wrote *Lessons in Comprehension: Explicit Instruction in the Reading Workshop* (Serafini, 2004), and in 2008 I published *More (Advanced) Lessons in Comprehension: Expanding Students' Understanding of All Types of Texts* (Serafini & Youngs, 2008), where I described in detail the explicit lessons that were an important component of my reading workshop. I wrote about the various resources, objectives, and artifacts I used to develop and conduct these lessons. Within each lesson contained in that book, I wrote about the actual language I used when conducting these lessons. The descriptions of the language I used for teaching these literary skills and concepts first focused my attention on the language of instruction and discussion.

After beginning with a "macro" view of the reading workshop, I narrowed the focus of my writing and observations to the actual lessons in comprehension conducted within the reading workshop. With this book, I narrow the focus even further, taking a "micro" view of the language used to conduct the comprehension lessons and literature discussions described in my earlier writings. This shift in perspective has taken me into some new areas of scholarship and fields of inquiry that focus on classroom discourse, discussions, and language. I have had an interesting couple of years studying this topic from a variety of perspectives. Before

I begin to describe in detail what I have learned and the instructional practices I recommend, I want to share some new insights that have emerged to inform my understandings as I prepared to write this book:

◆ First, the professional literature on language and classroom discourse is informed and investigated by a wide range of scholars and disciplines that goes beyond educational researchers and practitioners. In addition to educators, many other researchers—for example: anthropologists, sociologists, linguists, literary and critical theorists, speech therapists, and neuroscientists—are interested in language and its role in learning and teaching. Reading about classroom talk has taken me into new areas of scholarship to understand the vast influence language has on literacy education.

◆ Second, researchers have been studying classroom talk and analyzing it from a variety of perspectives for many years. However, there have been few books written about it that have had mass appeal for classroom teachers. Two influential discussions, Courtney Cazden's *Classroom Discourse* (1986) and Shirley Brice Heath's *Ways With Words: Language, Life and Work in Communities and Classrooms* (1983), were published in the 1980s. Although certainly not the first books to look at language in schools, they were two of the first books aimed at educators to focus on the language of teaching and learning. It is unfortunate that the body of knowledge focusing on classroom talk from a research and theoretical perspective is not better known among classroom teachers and teacher educators.

◆ Third, language has three primary functions. It has an ideational function; we use language to convey meanings, ideas, and understandings. It has an interpersonal or social function; that is, it develops and maintains relationships among people. Finally, it has an expressive function; that is, it plays a role in the construction of one's identity and helps people express attitudes and emotions. These three functions work simultaneously every time we talk with others. Specifically, as teachers are conveying ideas, they are also developing relationships with their students and expressing their identities while helping their students construct their own identities.

◆ Fourth, in the literature on classroom discourse, we have identified many types of teacher talk and we use multiple terms to describe these varieties. Terms such as *tentative talk, exploratory talk, dialogue,* and *shared contemplation,* to name just a few, are used to refer to very similar types of talk. I don't want readers of this book to get hung up on the various terms and jargon associated with these ideas and will do my best to remain consistent with the terms I choose, as well as expand on any new terms when they come along.

◆ Finally, and probably most important, the ways in which teachers talk and the language they use in classroom settings have actually changed very little in the past hundred years. How teachers talk to students and the types of questions they ask have been "institutionalized" through the various educational entities that prepare and support teachers. The traditional ways teachers talk have been supported by the models provided in the traditional methods classes teachers take. In addition, the movies we watch, the books we read, and the time we spent in school as students all affect the way we believe teachers should talk and classroom interactions should proceed. The expectations that people bring to the teaching profession have a profound effect on how they behave themselves and the language they use in their classrooms.

My "road to talk" has made me aware of the importance of focusing on both the big picture of the reading workshop and on the details and nuances of individual lessons in comprehension. In addition, my readings and classroom research have forced me to attend to the actual language teachers draw on during instruction and discussion and the ways it shapes how and what students learn, how they see themselves, and how willing they are to engage.

My Invitation

An introduction informs the reader of what lies ahead, and it should also tempt the reader to keep reading. I hope this one has done both. Come along with me as we explore some concepts and instructional practices that may at first glance seem inconsequential or obvious. I hope that by the end of this book you will become more aware of the language you use in your classroom and its effects on your students' learning, and that you will begin to attend to the nuances that various forms of talk play in the comprehension process.

CLASSROOM TALK
Why Do Teachers Talk the Way They Do?

I like to do all the talking myself.
It saves time and arguments.

—*Oscar Wilde*

Throughout our daily lives we use language to communicate our intentions and understandings, to foster relationships with other human beings, and to apprentice young children into our society. In and out of school settings, language is also used to scaffold the learning experiences of children and to regulate the complexity of the tasks they encounter, enabling them to do things they would not be able to do on their own. Through language, we create our identities and find our place in the world among ideas, peoples, and the artifacts and traditions of the cultures that have gone on before us.

In general, the language we use in educational settings and institutions is intended to help novices learn, teachers teach, and communities grow and thrive. For example, children learn through participation in classroom discussions the appropriate ways of talking about particular ideas, concepts, and fields of inquiry such as math, science, and literature. They learn how to interact with one another and the teacher. Particular ways of talking are endorsed in classrooms by teachers' responses to students, by the formal assessments we use to award grades and such, and by the expectations we set for the learning experiences we provide. In other words, through language children learn how to "do" school.

Teachers use language to sanction or endorse particular ways of talking and thinking that will help children succeed in various educational contexts. Children learn how to talk in specific ways by spending time talking with adults and other members of their communities. Students are apprenticed into ways of using language that make sense within particular social settings.

What this all means is that we use language to communicate as well as to make sense. Language is a "mediator" of our experiences with the world. In other words, it is through language that we make sense of the world and represent our own understandings of it. In school, we learn how to talk about literature by participating in literature discussions. Through language we learn how the game of school is played and what makes us successful at playing it. Of course, how well we play this game may have a tremendous impact on our future and the choices available throughout our lives. It's a wonder, with stakes as high as these, that classroom teachers aren't more concerned with how the specifics of language influence their teaching and students' learning.

Why Focus on Classroom Talk?

As I stated in the introduction to this book, talk is everywhere. It is our primary means of communicating and the means through which we come to know and understand our world. What more important reasons do we need for talking about talk? In 1984, John Goodlad wrote the classic *A Place Called School*, in which he described in fascinating detail his extensive observational research project of American public schools. Goodlad shared numerous insights about classroom discourse and the language teachers used during instruction. He explained how teachers did most of the talking throughout the school day, asked almost all of the questions, and controlled who spoke, when they spoke, and what they spoke about.

Almost 30 years after this monumental publication came out, my observations and classroom research would suggest that things haven't changed much in schools. Indeed, in many respects they have worsened. The advances that were made in the late 1980s and early 1990s focusing on teacher professionalism, teacher research, and teacher as instructional decision-maker have given way to state-sanctioned, mandated reading programs with instructional scripts and limited instructional decision-making for classroom teachers.

To believe that one can predetermine the language a teacher should use to teach effectively is naïve, if not arrogant and irresponsible. The language that enables teachers to explain something to students in the middle of a discussion or comprehension lesson is based on their ability to respond to the needs, interests, experiences, and abilities of a child in that moment, in that particular context. As teachers learn to pay attention to the language they use during instruction and discussions, they discover how their questions and response patterns shape the teaching and learning in their classrooms.

Try This! ▼ ▼ ▼

Rent a movie that takes place in a school and has scenes that show classroom instruction (e.g., *Teachers, Dangerous Minds,* or *Freedom Writers*). Analyze how the classrooms are arranged and the role of the teacher, paying close attention to the interaction patterns and the way teachers talk with their students. Try this also with children's novels that take place in school: *Bridge to Terabithia* (Paterson, 1977), *Frindle* (Clements, 1996), *The Landry News* (Clements, 1999), or *Nothing but the Truth* (Avi, 1991).

Interactive Discussions

James Dillon (1988) defines discussion as a particular form of group interaction in which members join together to address a question of common concern, exchanging and examining different views in service of enhancing their knowledge, decisions, or actions. This definition seems to get at the interactive nature of discussions, the type of engagement necessary for discussions to be successful, and the idea that quality discussions have a common focus or concern. The discussions we promote in our classrooms should foster student engagement around an area of common concern, while expanding the intellectual complexity of the topics under discussion. These two elements—engagement and intellectual complexity—are key elements in successful interactive discussions.

In order to explain the types of teacher talk that support engagement and intellectual complexity, I need to distinguish between teacher-directed talk and classroom talk in which students are more involved in the direction of the discussions. Teacher-directed talk is an authoritarian discourse, during which teachers control what is said, who gets to say what, and where the discussion is headed. This teacher-directed talk also refers to the traditional "chalk-and-talk" classroom lecture delivered daily from the front of the classroom. This type of teacher-directed talk also includes a particular way of asking questions we usually associate with traditional teaching. It is a "sit-and-get" teaching style, in which students are relegated to answering questions posed by the teacher driven by the goal to guess what is in the teacher's head, reminiscent of how Ben Stein, the actor who plays the teacher in the movie *Ferris Bueller's Day Off*, talks to his students.

In contrast to an authoritarian, teacher-directed discourse, collaborative talk is controlled by both teachers and students, allows for more than one person to pose and answer questions, and provides opportunities for more engaged participation by all members of the group. During interactive discussions, students play an integral role in determining the direction and focus of the discussion. To make discussions interactive, students need to be responsible for articulating their interpretations and ideas to the community of readers, for listening to what other students are saying, and for reconsidering what they are thinking. Members of interactive discussions assume an active role, listening intently to other students' ideas and interpretations and opening lines of communication among students rather than always going through the teacher.

Authoritarian or teacher-directed discourse generally

Characteristics of Interactive Classroom Discussion

Students assume these responsibilities:

* Articulating their own ideas and interpretations about their reading

* Listening actively to other students' ideas

* Opening lines of communication and negotiating meanings by responding directly to other students' understandings and interpretations

* Trying to understand what other students are saying

* Asking questions when ideas or concepts are unclear

* Remaining open to new ideas and opinions

focuses on the transmission of predetermined facts and concepts, not intellectual complexity and the expansion of readers' interpretive repertoires. In contrast, collaborative talk and interactive discussions create a space in the classroom for students to generate interpretations, articulate their ideas, and negotiate meanings with other readers.

Try This! ▾ ▾ ▾

Consider a time when you were in school and felt you were misunderstood. What role did language play in these feelings? How did you help others understand what you were trying to say? How did you use language to make your point? Often, people rely on metaphors or analogies to connect their ideas to their conversational partners' experiences. We use language to connect what we are trying to say with what we know our audience understands. The same is true in our classrooms. We can't simply say things again slower or louder to make ourselves understood. Teachers need to know how to connect new information with their students' experiences and how to draw on language to help their students relate and understand.

Traditional Classroom Interaction Patterns

Throughout the literature on classroom discourse, educators and researchers have juxtaposed a more traditional, authoritarian way of talking and teaching in classrooms with a more collaborative discourse style. The traditional way of interacting in classrooms is often referenced as the Initiate, Respond, and Evaluate

(IRE) pattern. This term was first used by Mehan (1979), Sinclair and Coulthard (1975), and Cazden (1986) in their writings during the 1970s and 1980s.

In the IRE pattern, teachers *initiate* a discussion topic, most frequently by posing a question to which students are expected to *respond*. Subsequently, teachers *evaluate* the response offered by students. In this interaction, teachers take turns speaking whenever they wish, decide what topics are important to discuss, determine who will talk and for how long, and interject their own responses and interpretations, controlling the pace and direction of the discussion.

Characteristics of IRE Discussions

* Teachers speak whenever they wish.
* Teachers allocate turns to others.
* Teachers determine topics.
* Teachers control pace of discussion.
* Teachers interrupt at will.
* Teachers pose questions at will.
* Teachers endorse particular readings.
* Teachers end conversational turns.

Before we continue, in order to give readers a sense of what an authoritarian discourse pattern looks like, I present a brief transcript from a third-grade classroom's discussion focusing on the classic picture book *Where the Wild Things Are* by Maurice Sendak (1963). Throughout this excerpt, the classroom teacher dominated the discussion (speaking more than 50 percent of the time), controlled the direction of the discussion by asking particular types of questions, and endorsed the responses of particular students that aligned with what she had predetermined to be important or correct. This transcript also demonstrates how students' responses are directly related to the questions and directives offered by the teacher, as students often simply "fill in the blanks" in the teacher's questions or directives (Wells, 1989).

To be clear, the inclusion of this transcript is not an attack on this teacher's qualifications or instructional abilities, nor do I consider the teacher to be a bad

CHAPTER 1 Classroom Talk: Why Do Teachers Talk the Way They Do?

19

teacher. On the contrary, I found her to be an excellent, caring, dedicated teacher who worked very hard to provide the best reading instruction she could for her students. What I hope this transcript demonstrates is the power of this traditional interaction pattern over teachers. It has been institutionalized as the appropriate way to talk and interact with students and represents what occurs in a majority of classrooms. After the transcript, I will discuss in greater detail why this interaction pattern is so embedded in classrooms and why teachers may find it so appealing. Throughout this book, all names used in the excerpts and transcripts are pseudonyms. The transcripts were taken from elementary and middle school classrooms that were part of various research projects conducted across the southwestern United States.

Teacher-Directed Discussion Example

Ms. B: [reading from the book *Where the Wild Things Are*] What is Max doing?

Jerry: He is starting to do things, like acting scary.

Ms. B: He's acting scary. What's he wearing? What's he wearing? Lonny, what's he wearing?

Lonny: A costume.

Ms. B: A costume. What kind of costume does it look like?

Lonny: A rabbit.

Ms. B: A rabbit? Are you sure? What do you think, Sarah? What does it look like he is wearing? What kind of costume?

Sally: A wolf suit.

Ms. B: Right, a wolf suit. Damien?

Damien: A wolf suit, because it said so in the words.

Ms. B: Right. [reading from the book again, emphasis on the words *wolf suit*] What is mischief? We talked about that. Keisha?

Keisha: Being bad.

Ms. B: Yeah, when you are doing mischief, are you doing what you are supposed to be doing?

Students: [chorally] No!

In this excerpt, the teacher assumed the role of arbiter of what is meaningful or correct, seemed to focus exclusively on the literal text, and directed the discussion toward particular meanings and answers. The answers were often found directly in the written text, not in what the readers brought to the text. A primary goal of this authoritarian discourse is the transfer of knowledge and information from teacher to students. In an IRE interaction, teachers directly control the discussions and lead students to the answers they often predetermine or prefer.

In another example of an IRE interaction, the teacher is discussing the picture book *The Three Pigs* (Wiesner, 2001) with her fourth-grade class. It becomes obvious after listening to this discussion that she had something in particular in mind that she wanted her students to consider and respond to.

Ms. S: What would you like to say about the pigs, Sammy?

Sammy: The pigs have a shirt on in the pictures.

Ms. S: Is there a shirt there?

Michael: No, that's a stripe.

Ms. S: Okay, does it matter if he has a shirt or a stripe?

Students: No!

Ms. S: How many of you think that this pig in the picture is the same one on the other page? [students all raise hands] Okay, so what is going on here? Why are the pictures like that?

Jorge: Because the author likes to use different colors in his books.

Ms. S: Just because he likes colors? I think there is more to it. Anybody else have another idea? Why is it like that, Louis?

Louis: Maybe because he got bored with only one way of drawing.

Ms. S: Oh, come on, students! The illustrator is doing something with the illustrations. What is he doing?

Sharon: He is trying to show us something.

Ms. S: Yes, he is trying to show something. What is he showing us?

Gerald: I have no idea.

Ms. S: Okay, let me explain. When the pigs go from one picture to another, they are going from one story to another, and the illustrator is showing that they are changing stories. Get it?

Students: [all together] Yes, Ms. S.

IRE discussions often have a predetermined focus that doesn't change in response to what students are saying. Regardless of what the students were saying, the teacher had a focus and purpose for this discussion, and she used questions and statements to lead students to her point. This by itself isn't necessarily a bad thing, but we need to understand how this affects discussions, and how the language we use supports—or hinders—our students' own thinking and interpretations.

Kris Gutierrez (Gutierrez, Rymes, & Larson, 1995) described this way of talking as a form of "recitation script," in which students simply recite what they think the teacher wants them to say, limiting opportunities for students to engage in the discussion, interact directly with other students, or construct their own questions. Courtney Cazden (1986) has described the IRE pattern as a "default setting," implying that without deliberate attention to one's language and patterns of interacting with students, teachers will default to this way of talking due to the lure of "tradition," many years of apprenticeship in this ritualized "school form of interaction," and its idealization as the most effective way to discuss and deliver the curriculum. We now need to consider why this type of interaction, this way of talking, has become institutionalized throughout the teaching profession and why it seems so appealing to classroom teachers.

Try This! ▼ ▼ ▼

Record a classroom discussion and listen to the recording. Listen carefully to your role as teacher. If you have time, transcribe a brief section of the recording by typing your talk in red and students' talk in black. Does the transcript suggest a "back-and-forth" interaction like the one described above? How many questions did you ask? Were there times when more than one student responded in a row? Consider how your students and you, in turn, responded.

Why Is This Way of Talking So Appealing?

There are numerous reasons why the traditional classroom interaction appeals to classroom teachers. Historically, classroom management has been a primary focus in teacher preparation programs and remains a large part of the evaluation systems used to assess the quality of teacher candidates. Good teaching equals a controlled classroom, and IRE interactions allow for more teacher control. This interaction pattern is also appealing because teachers can use it to determine which topics are worth discussing, the extent to which individual students participate, and the responses that will be sanctioned as important or correct. One may also conclude that the pressures of trying to "cover the curriculum" lead teachers to this way of interacting with students and asking questions.

Other tensions that affect the dominant patterns of classroom interaction in literacy education and instruction:

1. *The pacing of a lesson and time allowed for students to ponder or explore new interpretations.* Teachers feel pressure to "keep moving" during lessons, and even more so during discussions. Until teachers and curriculum designers begin to value the role of talk and the impact it has on learning, teachers will do the majority of it and limit the amount of time dedicated to student talk.

2. *The search for a single main idea.* As long as teachers think there is a single, universal meaning in a text, their classroom discussions will focus on trying to find it. Teachers need to recognize a variety of acceptable, viable interpretations for any text and allow for students to share and consider what these may be.

3. *Apprenticeship into a particular way of talking through years of watching it.* Teachers learn to talk and act like the models they were provided as they were learning to teach. Whether it is from a book, a movie, or a classroom observation, we learn to talk like the people we hear speaking.

4. *Lack of experience with the content being discussed.* It's hard to talk deeply about things we don't understand! If they want to support more sophisticated discussions, teachers need to be able to read and understand the texts they share in their classrooms more deeply. According to a study by Hoewisch (2000), very few teacher licensure programs across the United States require a course in children's literature anymore. This is unfortunate. How can we expect teachers to talk deeply about things they don't understand and can't talk about themselves?

5. *Focus on control.* One of the most influential factors in how teachers talk with students is their need to control their classrooms and discussions. We take entire courses on classroom management, and commercial programs offer strategies for discipline and behavior control. However, rigid teacher control often leads to a decrease in student participation. The more we control what

students say, the less chance we have of hearing what they are actually saying and thinking.

It is not surprising, nor is it teachers' fault, that they learn to emulate particular ways of talking with their students. The purpose of this book is to call teachers' attention to the ways they talk and the ways in which their talk affects what happens in classrooms and in students' learning.

Why Is This Way of Interacting a Problem?

One may ask why, since we are the product of traditional classrooms and managed to succeed, our students shouldn't benefit from similar instruction and discussions. To address this issue, we need to consider what the objectives of literacy education are, and what the research on effective practice reveals.

To begin, this is not an "all-or-nothing" question. There may, in fact, be times when we want to ask literal questions and have students simply recite concepts or answers to our questions. However, there are probably more times when we don't. The questions we ask and the interactions we support have different effects on students' comprehension and understandings. When we limit what students can say, we limit how they think. I don't believe any teacher would ever deliberately limit a student's thinking. However, until we consciously attend to how we interact and talk with students, we may inadvertently be holding our students back.

Authoritarian, teacher-directed discourse affects how students interact in classrooms and how they comprehend the texts they encounter. Here are several challenges associated with an authoritarian discourse we may want to consider:

1. *Reducing comprehension to literal recall.* There are times when focusing exclusively on the literal text limits what students can discuss and, in effect, limits their comprehension of a text. Too often, the text is seen as the sole focus of a discussion. We point to the text as the container of all meaning. This assumes that the words on the page refer to meanings that we all agree on and that will remain stable across time. We have all read a book at different times, or with different students, and reached different understandings. The

literal text alone cannot account for this. In Chapter 2, I'll share an in-depth exploration of what is meant by reading comprehension.

2. *Teacher-directed talk focuses on reaching consensus, rather than exploring possibilities.* What is interesting in discussions is not what we all agree on, but those comments that help us explore new ideas and nudge us to reconsider what we think. It is important that we realize we don't all have to agree to understand something. It is through the sharing and reconsideration of new ideas that we learn and grow.

3. *The focus remains on what teachers say, rather than on how students listen and respond.* There is a difference when we look at what is learned, rather than simply what is taught or spoken. We need to consider not only how teachers talk but also how students listen and respond. Teachers and commercial publishers cannot script in advance what students will say. They must pay attention to what students say and remain sensitive to what this means for their students' comprehension processes.

4. *What it means to be fully literate has expanded.* Literal recall may help students do well on standardized tests, but it won't help them fully participate as literate citizens in today's society. The literacy demands placed on today's students are far more complex than the demands of the early 1900s. There was a time when simply being able to sign one's name meant you were literate and were allowed to vote and own land. Literacy in today's society is infinitely more complex.

In contrast to the teacher-directed, authoritarian discourse described above, another way of talking and interacting with students is possible. Too often, teachers think that if they give up control, or share control with students, their classes will become chaotic. Sharing control does not mean we give it up; it just means that both teachers and students have more involvement in these discussions and interactions. It is to this interactive, collaborative classroom discussion we now turn.

Interactive Comprehension Strategies: Fostering Meaningful Talk About Text

CHAPTER 2

PREFERRED VISION

Setting New Expectations for Classroom Interactions

When we find ourselves in the majority,
we may want to reconsider our position.

—*Mark Twain*

Just because we have always talked to students in particular ways and asked certain types of questions does not mean that those ways of talking are the most effective. Tradition and institutions have tremendous power over the way we do things. We see and hear teachers talking in certain ways with students during our student teaching experiences, in movies and books about schools, and in our conversations with other teachers. Just because everyone is doing it doesn't mean that it is effective or supportive of students' learning and thinking. The demonstrations we experience showing how teachers are expected to talk have a lasting effect on how we interact with our students in our own classrooms.

To change the way we talk with students, we need to be able to envision a new, preferred way of talking. Developing this *preferred vision* for our classroom interactions requires that we imagine a different way of interacting with our students. We should invest time in watching other teachers interact with students in more effective ways, read research and professional books about why we may want to rethink how we talk with our students, enjoy opportunities to talk with other teachers about these changes, and explore new ways of interacting with students in our own classrooms.

Developing a Preferred Vision

A preferred vision requires us to imagine a different way of doing things. It requires us to move "outside the box" of traditional classroom interaction patterns. An effective way to begin this process is to record our own discussions on audio- or videotape and critically examine the language we use and its effects on our literacy instruction and literature discussions. As mentioned earlier, we tend to default to a traditional way of talking when we don't closely attend to how we talk and respond to students. Conscious attention to our language enables us to monitor and change, as needed, the interactions that occur in our classrooms.

Try This! ▼ ▼ ▼

Record a 15-minute discussion focusing on a poem, short story, or picture book. Listen to the recording while alone and ask yourself the following questions:

1. How did you begin the session and introduce the book? What expectations or objectives did you set for the experience?

2. Did you ask questions, make statements, or accept comments during the reading of the book, or did you wait until you were finished for most of the discussion? In other words, how did you balance the flow of the story with your desire to allow students to comment on the story?

3. How many questions did you ask during the discussion? What types of questions were asked? Literal? Inferential? (See Chapter 4 for details.)

4. What types of responses did students have to your questions and comments? Personal connections? Noticings? Wonderings?

5. Did students talk with one another during the discussion or just with you?

6. What would you have done differently now that you have analyzed this discussion?

After thinking about your discussion, honestly consider how close your interactions were to the traditional way of talking and whether there was any evidence of your trying new ways of talking with your students. Developing a preferred vision requires us to be honest about what we have been doing and reconsider its effects on our students' thinking and learning. Developing a preferred vision nudges us to examine our objectives for a particular discussion or lesson and make judgments about what we consider worthwhile. A preferred vision asks us to critically examine current practices based on our expectations for the future.

Characteristics of Effective Teachers

As our vision of effective teaching grows, so does our vision of the types of interactions we prefer. In a sense, developing a preferred vision requires us as teachers to continually develop and revise our conception of an effective teacher. To that end, I offer the following characteristics of an effective teacher:

- ▲ Possesses rich and flexible knowledge of academic content
- ▲ Understands how students develop ideas and concepts
- ▲ Is able to enact effective instructional practices
- ▲ Focuses on the role of language during instruction and discussions
- ▲ Uses flexible groupings to address individual students' needs
- ▲ Embeds instruction in authentic literacy tasks and environments
- ▲ Provides access to a wide variety of quality resources
- ▲ Utilizes a variety of assessments to understand students' needs and abilities
- ▲ Achieves higher levels of student involvement
- ▲ Creates effective classroom environments for learning
- ▲ Conducts inquiry into her/his own teaching

Effective teachers vary greatly in their teaching practices, but the research is quite compelling regarding some of the general characteristics listed above. Effective teachers engage students. On one hand, it's really that simple; on the other, it's more complicated. Language and activities are the two primary means we use to engage students in learning experiences. We have all seen or experienced the teacher who drones on and on, putting students slowly to sleep. This is a language issue as much as a content issue. It doesn't matter how interested students are in a particular subject; if we can't talk effectively with them about this material, they won't engage.

Interactive Comprehension Strategies: Fostering Meaningful Talk About Text

In addition to these characteristics of effective teachers, teachers need time to observe other teachers and talk about what they observe. To support these observations and discussions, principals and instructional leaders or literacy specialists need to provide time for teachers to visit other classrooms and discuss what they are observing. We need to break down the walls of isolation that often accompany our profession. We need to encourage teachers to question their teaching practices and philosophies and provide opportunities for them to step back and reflect on their teaching. This "stepping back," or achieving some distance from one's teaching, requires that we find ways to see ourselves "on the stage" as teachers. We can accomplish this through journal-writing focusing on our own teaching, sharing observational notes of others' teaching, and recording and analyzing our own teaching using audio and video technologies.

Try This! ▼ ▼ ▼

In your teacher lounge, or during a staff meeting at the beginning of the year, create a T-chart that includes "Things I Want to See" and "Things I'm Willing to Share," like the one in Figure 2.1 below. Invite teachers to add some suggestions to either column. The principal is then responsible for finding ways to get teachers release time to visit other classrooms or demonstrate what they do well. This does two important things: it respects the knowledge of the teachers in the school, and it helps break down the walls of isolation among our teachers.

Things I Want to See	Things I'm Willing to Share

▲ Figure 2.1: Teacher demonstrations chart

Language of Instruction vs. Language of Discussion

This book focuses on two types of classroom talk: the language used during literature discussions and the language of comprehension instruction. It's not that one type of language is inherently better than the other; it's just that they are different and do different things. Therefore, we need to be sure that we are using the language that supports the objectives of comprehension instruction or literature discussions.

Comprehension lessons focus on teaching strategies and skills for making sense of a variety of texts. These lessons often involve teachers sharing cognitive strategies such as visualizing, summarizing, making inferences, and so on. Literature discussions involve teachers and students sharing their responses to and analyses of a particular text. During these discussions teachers and students share personal connections, things they notice in the text and images, and any questions that may arise. This difference in the objectives for each of these learning experiences requires a shift in language. Looking at a comparison chart (see Figure 2.2) may help reveal the differences between these two types of language use.

Language of Instruction	Language of Discussion
Call to attention/focus	Invitations to participate
Explicitness	Tentativeness
Explanatory talk	Exploratory talk
Appropriate pacing	Allowance for students' divergences
Focus on objectives	Focus on possibilities
Responses used to confirm	Responses used to extend

▲ Figure 2.2: Language of instruction and discussions

This chart refers to some of the characteristics that I have observed in classrooms during explicit comprehension lessons and during literature discussions. The primary differences focus on teacher direction and the extent and nature of student involvement. During instruction, teachers tend to use explicit language that focuses students' attention on particular aspects of reading, relates to the objectives of the lesson, and explains what students are doing or should be doing. The language of instruction is concerned with maintaining an appropriate pace and telling students whether their responses are heading in the right direction.

Try This! ▾ ▾ ▾

Record an explicit lesson in comprehension and another of a literature study discussion. Listen to the two recordings and think about the roles you adopted in each setting. Ask yourself:

1. In which setting did you talk more and ask more questions?

2. What types of comments did you make in each setting and how did they differ?

3. How much did students talk in each setting? Did they talk more in one than in the other?

4. Think about your purpose for each instructional experience. Did the language you use support your purpose, or did it hinder students' participation and understandings?

In contrast, the language of discussion encourages students to participate and share their thoughts and opinions. This language is more tentative, and teachers are more cautious about sharing their opinions and interpretations. Rather than explicitly transmitting ideas, concepts, and interpretations to students, the language we use in discussions encourages our students to explore new ideas, to wonder and wander in their thinking, to focus on various possibilities, and to extend their ideas in new and interesting ways. I refer to this talk as *collaborative* or *interactive*. What are its characteristics?

Interactive Discussions and Collaborative Talk

During an interactive discussion students are responsible for articulating their thoughts, interpretations, and ideas to other students. This allows for a multiplicity of voices. It's difficult to have a discussion when no one is sharing ideas or when students aren't listening to one another. To support interactive discussions, then, we need to help students learn how to become active listeners. In general, active listeners look at the person speaking, use gestures to acknowledge participation, consider what other speakers offer, and incorporate others' ideas into their own thinking.

In addition to having students and teachers learn how to be active listeners, we want to ensure that the lines of communication during our discussions are from student to student as well as from student to teacher. Too often, students only respond to the teacher, even when they may be addressing another student. We need to be careful that students don't try to speak through us to other students. There are times in our discussions when it's appropriate to tell students to turn and look at another student as they are responding to his or her ideas. Teachers are a dominating presence in literature discussions, and we need to find ways to reduce students' tendencies to speak directly to us—and only to us.

In 2006, Robin Alexander, a British educator and researcher, offered the following five characteristics of collaborative talk:

1. Collective—teachers and students learn and address issues together

2. Reciprocal—teachers and students listen to one another, share ideas

3. Supportive—students articulate ideas freely without fear of reprisal

4. Cumulative—teachers and students build on one another's ideas

5. Purposeful—teachers steer talk with educational goals in mind

These five characteristics help us envision a way of talking with students that goes beyond simple recitation and engages them in determining the direction and content of the classroom discussions. Alexander's five characteristics of classroom discussions suggest that in the most effective discussions teachers and students should work together to generate understandings in a supportive environment.

Let me share with you an example of an interactive discussion before we continue. In this discussion, the teacher is sharing several books the class has been exploring during a unit of study focusing on complex picture books. Some of these picture books have multiple story lines or narrators, a variety of perspectives, and unusual design features. The discussion took place in a fifth-grade class that had already read several of the books.

Mr. J: Okay, yeah. Talk to me about these books.

Alex: This book [*The Three Pigs*] is like *The Stinky Cheese Man* because the narrator interrupted the story.

Mr. J: How does that book compare to this one?

Morgan: In *The Three Pigs*, the narrator and all the characters are in their own world.

Valerie: They're not in the same story world.

Mr. J: It's as if they're real. They have their own existence. Like they are actors performing for a different story.

Chandler: Kind of like *Bad Day at Riverbend* because it's almost like when the girl is coloring the pictures. It's out in the real world and in the book world. They don't know what's going on in the other worlds.

Allison: David Wiesner wrote them both. Ever since the pigs took to the air at the end of his book *Tuesday*, Wiesner has wanted to give them a book of their own.

Savannah: Maybe the pigs escaped from there.

Mr. J: Are you saying the pigs in this story escaped from the book *Tuesday*?

Jason: The pigs look a lot alike, too.

Mr. J: Okay, so you all think the pigs escaped from *Tuesday* and went to *The Three Pigs*. Remember at the beginning, he wanted to make sure the pigs got to tell their version of the story. Dylan?

Dylan: It's kind of like where *Why the Chicken Crossed the Road* ended, *Black and White* picked up. Then, where *Tuesday* ended, this one [*The Three Pigs*] picked up with the pigs. I think he does this in his books.

Mr. J: Yeah? Do you all think that *Black and White* picked up where *Why the Chicken Crossed the Road* ended? Personally, I can't see it. You've got to show me your ideas. I'm not saying you're wrong, I just want you to show me some evidence. You guys have great insight into books and see things that I don't. But I am not sure about this interpretation yet.

Chandler: I think the pigs felt like they were free when they were out of the story. Also, even though they give their names, they don't use names at all. He doesn't use them.

Mr. J: Why do you think they felt free? That's an interesting word to use.

Jason: They were away from the wolf.

Mr. J: You have taken them outside this story and have given them a life of their own. They were stuck in the *Three Pigs* story. You kind of have to keep going back and forth with this break in reality of the story. So they wouldn't get eaten. At the same time, they could visit any story they want. It's kind of hard to hang in there with that idea that these pigs are fictional characters yet they're real and free, roaming and talking, too.

Andrew: I think Wiesner dedicated it to David Macaulay because I think David Macaulay inspired him to write the book because one thing leads to another.

In this discussion transcript, two points stand out. The first is a more equitable sharing of "talking time" by the teacher and the students. As we saw earlier, in IRE discussions, teacher talk dominates the conversation. In this discussion, the students' voices are heard. Second, the teacher respects the students' contributions. Although he doesn't always agree with the students, he respects their right to disagree and encourages them to think about their interpretations in light of the available evidence. Finally, although the discussion has a focus, it does not seem that the teacher is simply leading the students to a predetermined meaning or destination. The direction of the discussion is open for negotiation. Together, students and teacher will take the discussion in directions that serve their purposes and needs, not simply the teacher's agenda.

Setting Expectations for Interactive Discussions

To facilitate more effective discussions, we cannot simply sit back and hope that our students understand what we expect them to do when we discuss a text. We need to make our expectations for interactive discussions clear and explicit, sharing our ideas and preferred vision with our students if we expect them to participate in particular ways. When we share our expectations with our students, we help them understand the purposes and procedures for these interactions. I list below some expectations that I would share with my students early in the school year to help set the tone for our discussions.

Honest Reporting

Expecting students to share what they honestly think and feel is the most important goal we can set for our students; otherwise, our discussions are doomed to fail. We need to develop a sense of community in our classrooms that makes students feel comfortable enough to share their thoughts with honesty and integrity. I have suggested during my professional development workshops that we need to allow students to feel comfortable enough to tell us that they hate our favorite book—and, even more important, why they dislike it. If they feel comfortable enough to do that, maybe they will share their honest reactions to the other texts we read and share.

Listening Well and Thinking Deeply Are as Important as Talking

Successful discussions require people to share ideas, but they also require people to listen to what has been said and to think about these ideas. Students involve themselves in the life of our classrooms in different ways. Some offer ideas frequently, while others are more reticent to share what they think. In our desire to get students to share their thoughts, we can't forget that those students who aren't sharing every day may be listening carefully and considering what has been discussed.

Students Involve Themselves in the Discussion in Various Ways

We need to find multiple ways for everyone to share their ideas. For example, having students turn to a partner and share their thoughts with one person before sharing with the whole class ensures that everyone has an opportunity to speak and be heard. The more response channels we offer, the more voices we will hear.

Students Address One Another as Well as the Teacher

Too often, students speak through us to other students rather than directly to one another. We don't want to position ourselves in our discussions as the hub through which all talk flows. When a student disagrees or agrees with another student, he or she needs to talk to that student, not through us. Seating arrangements that allow students to see one another is a good way to encourage this type of interaction.

Half-Baked Ideas Are Accepted and Encouraged

We cannot wait until our students have "fully baked" their ideas before they are willing to offer them. I like it when students tentatively offer their ideas, sharing their thought processes and current thinking. For example, when students say, "I'm kind of thinking that maybe the main character in the story should not have acted the way she did because she hurt other people," you get a sense of their thinking in process. Ideally, our discussions will support our students' thinking in process and not just their final interpretations.

Students Consider What Has Been Offered by Other Students

Listening to other students helps all students consider the flow of ideas, questions, and comments. Sometimes the ideas our students offer seem to be disjointed—that is, they don't seem to have paid attention to what has been said and what has previously been shared. We want students to take up from what has been shared and move the discussion in new directions.

Everyone Is Willing to Reconsider Their Ideas

Coming to a discussion unwilling to consider what other people think and reluctant to change one's mind can doom classroom discussions. We want students to enter our classroom discussions with open minds and honest ideas, ones that they are passionate about, but, at the same time, with a willingness to consider their peers' ideas.

Every year, I set out to create a caring, democratic classroom environment in which my students feel empowered to speak out about issues that really matter to them and where their personal experiences and interpretations are heard and considered by all members of our classroom community. A classroom environment that is both challenging and supportive—where students feel free to express popular and unpopular interpretations and opinions—is our goal. We aim to create a space where our students reflect basic respect for all individuals in the community, even during times of intellectual challenge.

Impediments to Interactive Discussions

Despite the expectations we set and the demonstrations of interactive discussions we offer, there are impediments to achieving more collaborative, interactive discussions. As much as we try to encourage students to pay close attention and listen to one another, sometimes our best intentions go awry. I offer a "top 10 list" of impediments to achieving interactive discussions.

10. Dominating Voices

When only two or three people are heard each day, our discussions are limited in their effectiveness. Some students talk constantly, which is fine, unless it limits the voices of other students.

9. Passive Participants

You can't have dominating voices unless the participants allow other students to dominate the discussion. We have to work with our students to engage them in our discussions and encourage them to share their voices.

8. Lack of Time

It's difficult to have an in-depth discussion on any substantial topic in two minutes. We need to provide extended periods of time for students to share and consider ideas. As we begin to understand the importance of discussions, we dedicate more time to this classroom experience.

7. Focus on "Winning" the Discussion

The goal of an interactive discussion is to illuminate and expand students' understandings, not prove someone wrong. When discussions focus on the gaps in thinking rather than helping other students understand what was read, the effectiveness of our discussions is limited.

6. Emphasis on Consensus

The most interesting part of literature discussions is the possibilities that new interpretations offer participants. Concepts such as "main idea" force students to compromise their ideas in order to agree with the teacher and other students. An effective discussion does not require students to agree. We all need to learn to tolerate the ambiguity of ideas in our classroom discussions to allow for more possibilities and a range of interpretations.

5. Defensive Attitudes

Effective interactive discussions are not for the meek and faint of heart. One must be ready to share and defend ideas in a supportive context. If students are afraid of sharing ideas and of being challenged to support their thoughts, discussions are less effective.

4. Attacks on Others

There is no place for personal attacks in classroom discussions. If one student dismisses another by suggesting his or her ideas are stupid or worthless, that is, in my opinion, grounds for immediate removal from the classroom. Respect and trust form the core of lively discussions; ridicule has no role.

3. Failure to Listen to Others

Fruitful discussions rely on active listening. It is in the sharing and reconsidering of ideas that we grow and develop our own interpretive abilities. This begins with attentive and sensitive listening.

2. Inability to Consider Alternative Perspectives

Empathy and the ability to understand another's perspective is an important component of effective interactive discussions. The best discussions take place when participants understand and appreciate views that differ from their own. And while they respect another student's perspective, they may not necessarily agree with it.

I. Lack of Experience With Texts

Simply put, it's hard to facilitate an effective discussion about a particular text when we don't understand the text ourselves. The more we analyze literature ourselves, the better positioned we will be to support the interpretations and analyses of our students.

We need to figure a way around these impediments if we are to ensure that our discussions are interactive, not authoritarian. These impediments are as much about our own challenges as teachers as they are characteristics of the students we encounter in our classrooms. As we call students' attention to the challenges and expectations for our interactive discussions, we begin to break down the impediments to more effective discussions.

Expanding Discussions— Expanding Comprehension

The opening epigraph of this book establishes the primary goal of expanding the thinking and talking that occurs in the reading workshop. The purpose for this expansion of thinking is to create and support readers who comprehend what they read. To expand the types of talk about texts that occur in our classrooms, we might do well to rethink our understanding of comprehension.

I believe that comprehension is a process of actively constructing meaning in transaction with texts in a particular social context. Comprehension is concerned with how viable interpretations are, how interpretations become useful, and how they are warranted or endorsed by a community of readers. In other words, we need to consider which meanings created by our students are allowed to count.

There are multiple meanings and interpretations that arise in transactions with texts, some viable, some not. In our interactive discussions, the viability of a particular interpretation is discussed, challenged, endorsed, and allowed to count. Reading-comprehension instruction should focus on understanding texts from a variety of perspectives and learning how these perspectives endorse and dismiss particular meanings and interpretations. For readers to construct meaning in transaction with texts, they must understand the codes and conventions of written language, become familiar with the vocabulary used by the author, and connect the text with their own experiences and background knowledge. This is the essence of comprehension.

Closing Comments

Language brings the ideas in our heads together with the concepts that exist in the world. Through language, our students learn to articulate their ideas and hear the responses of other students. When we create spaces in our reading workshops for students to share their interpretations and ponder the thoughts of others, the possibilities for intellectual development abound.

Teachers use language to regulate the complexity of a learning experience for their students. In other words, through language, teachers can support students doing things they could not do on their own. In addition, it is through language that we enact the curriculum. We use language to teach those concepts and skills we are required to teach. The curriculum guides we are given at the beginning of the year do not get up in front of the class and teach students by themselves! As teachers, we are responsible for understanding the content of the guides and enacting the curriculum, and we do all of this through the language we employ and the experiences we design. Debra Myhill and colleagues (Myhill, Jones, & Hopper, 2006) remind us that it is too easy to plan interactive discussions and experiences only to have them become authoritarian or teacher-controlled experiences in their delivery. Our challenge goes beyond revising lesson plans—we must pay attention to our talk with our students. Becoming aware of the language we use in our lessons and classroom discussions is our best defense against regressing into traditional, authoritarian interaction patterns that are waiting to spring back into action. This way of talking creates passive students and reduces the possibilities for extending and refining students' thinking and comprehension processes. Martin Nystrand (1997) suggests that instruction is orderly but lifeless when the teacher predetermines most of its content, scope, and direction, and this lifeless curriculum fosters student passivity.

Robert Scholes (1985) maintains there is a bright little student inside most teachers who wants to set the rest of the class straight, because he or she knows the "right answer." He further suggests it is our job not to intimidate students with our own superior textual interpretations, but to show them the codes upon which all textual interpretation depends and to encourage their own textual interpretations.

We will want to choose conversational patterns that support thinking and intellectual complexity, not just simple literal recall and recitation. Our goal is to strive for a language that supports "mindfulness," one that sets high expectations for our students and challenges them to think in complex and novel ways. Robin Alexander (2006) stated that talk is essential for the intellectual and social development of all children. For some children, the talk in which they engage at school is nothing less than a lifeline. It is through talk that we create and re-create our identities, develop relationships with others, come to understand the world, and share our experiences with others. In other words, it is through language that we become who we are. What else could be more important?

INTERACTIVE DISCUSSIONS

Getting Beyond "I Like the Book!"

Language is designed for doing something much
more interesting than transmitting information
accurately from one brain to another; it allows
people to make better sense of the world.

—*Neil Mercer (2000)*

How many of us have heard, as we sat down to discuss a book with our students,
"I liked the book" or "I didn't like the book"? Often, in our hurry to get to more
important aspects of the text, we rush past these judgments to ask, "Why did you
like the book?" only to be confronted with shrugged shoulders and a dismissive "I

don't know." As much as I like to get beyond personal judgments about books and into students' analyses and interpretations, we cannot assume these initial reactions or judgments aren't important aspects of our discussions.

Indeed, these initial reactions may serve the same role as the introductory conversation that often occurs when we enter a party. Our greetings and welcoming statements position us alongside other members of our community. When we arrive at a party, we begin by talking with our host and fellow partygoers about the weather, the health of their family members, the condition of our lawn, or outcomes of recent sporting events. We may eventually be drawn into a discussion about the challenges of parenthood, a recent divorce, or some other pressing concern, but to bypass the opening greetings and niceties would be considered rude. It is the same way with literature discussions.

From preschool to graduate school, students begin their discussions by stating whether they liked a book, what parts they liked and disliked, and the experience they had reading the text. With time and skillful facilitation, they may have the opportunity to share their interpretations and critiques of a particular book, but this is later, after the niceties have been exchanged. These welcoming statements are just as important when we join a literature study group as they are when we enter a social gathering.

However, a problem arises when the chitchat ("I liked the book") is as far as students get. Due to time constraints, lack of preparation, or simply the inability to facilitate a discussion beyond this point, teachers are sometimes unable to help students get past their initial reactions, personal judgments, and recall of literal events to analysis, interpretation, and critique.

The challenge for teachers is learning how to gently nudge students beyond the literal text and personal judgments without perceiving these initial experiences as inconsequential or unimportant. I want my students to react and respond to the books I read. I want them to like the books I choose to share with them and house in our classroom library. I want them to get excited and emotionally involved in what is being shared. But I also want them to move into interpretation and analysis of what has been read. The challenge is how to "up the ante" without dismissing students' initial reactions and personal judgments.

Teaching Techniques That Help Kids Find Their Voice

In his wonderful book *Choice Words*, Peter Johnston (2004) asks teachers to use language that is "powerful enough to change behavior" but "without force." In other words, we can't bully students into responding or thinking. We have to entice children into considering literature, invite them to share their ideas, and find ways to respond to their efforts that foster their engagement and interpretations of what has been read. Interactive discussion techniques—coupled with basic understandings about effective teaching—are designed to help kids know we value their voices, opinions, and ideas.

Getting the Floor

When we encourage students to raise their hands to show us they have something to say, it places control of the discussion firmly in our hands. This means that only those we call on get a chance to participate. There are times when we may want this to be the case, when we want to have control over who is speaking, but there are consequences worth considering when we use this approach during literature discussions.

When we require students to raise their hands to signal their intentions, we also allow them to "tune out" until we call their name. By raising their hands, students learn they don't have to listen to what is being said; they only have to listen for their name. When a teacher calls on a specific student, the teacher and the student, then, may be the only ones involved in the discussion. This certainly is not the nature of the interactions we hope to establish in our literature discussions.

We alter the dynamics of classroom interactions in a positive way once we get past the initial challenge of teaching children how to "get the floor." When students are required to listen for openings or pauses during a discussion that signal it's polite to enter, they are forced to attend to what is being said. To "get the floor," students must focus on what is being said to learn when to offer their ideas. Learning to make this work takes time, numerous demonstrations, lots of patience, and some help and encouragement from the teacher. But when it does work, the discussions are more dynamic and less teacher-directed. This allows for more student voices to be heard and forces students to become active listeners.

Try This! ▼ ▼ ▼

It takes time to help students learn how to enter a conversation without raising their hands or being called on to talk. Ask students to try taking turns talking after you finish reading a book. Show them how to wait their turn and allow others to speak first. The best way to know when it is polite to speak is by paying close attention to the person speaking. When they have finished, a space opens for other students to step in. It takes time to learn conversational turn-taking, and occasionally students will speak over one another. The best way to overcome this challenge is to work with students on listening and allowing others a chance to speak. Successful turn-taking begins and ends with active listening.

CHAPTER 3   Interactive Discussions: Getting Beyond "I Like the Book!"

49

I Can See You!

Another general consideration is the physical arrangement of the classroom and the proximity of the students to one another and the teacher during discussions. By moving students into positions where they can see one another, rather than having them sitting in rows staring at the backs of other students' heads, we can change the dynamics of our classroom discussions.

There is something about seeing one another when we are discussing a book that fosters more engagement and interaction. Sociologists have noted that the introduction of the television into the American household created physical arrangements that forever changed the way people interact in their homes. We moved from a circular setup, exemplified by the dining room table, to a linear arrangement, where all seats face the same direction, specifically toward the television. While this arrangement may be effective for watching television, it does not foster interaction.

The same holds true for the physical arrangements of our classrooms. If all of our students are facing us, they will have a harder time interacting with one another. For example, middle and high school teachers often share their concerns about getting students to talk about the books they have read. Due to their departmentalized schedules and the large number of students per class, middle and high school teachers often arrange students' desks in rows all facing the teacher's desk. This may work well for the lecture and presentation aspects of their teaching but does not foster the kind of student-to-student interaction that underlies rich discussion about reading. Simply asking students not to raise their hands while they are sitting in rows may not achieve the desired results.

Having students change their seating arrangements signals a different interaction pattern. They learn that when they sit in a circle the teacher expects them to talk to one another and join the discussion in different ways. The physical arrangement changes how students participate and signals a different set of expectations for their involvement. If we expect students to talk with one another, rather than just back and forth with the teacher, we need to rearrange our classrooms to support student-to-student interaction.

We cannot underestimate the power of place and physical arrangements in supporting our discussions. While traveling through Italy, I became cognizant of how people changed their tone of voice and conversational styles as they entered various cathedrals from the adjacent piazzas. Their voices were lowered and the tone become more respectful as they crossed the threshold of the church. Place affects behavior. We can take advantage of this understanding as we organize for our discussions by using place and physical arrangements to signal to students how we want them to talk and interact. The circular "dinner table" arrangement—students grouped in a circle—seems to foster student-to-student interaction.

Try This! ▼ ▼ ▼

Draw a floor plan of your classroom and consider how to rearrange it to accommodate a circle or semicircle for discussions. Teaching students to move their desks quickly or to get up and sit on the floor in an orderly fashion facilitates these arrangements. I often play a song on my CD player (approximately two minutes long) to signal this transition. Once students become accustomed to the length of time they have to make a transition, they learn to move quickly and efficiently.

We Are in This Together

Another general consideration is the use of the first-person plural "we" when talking with students. I like talking with my students as follows: "We need to reconsider our thoughts about the character in this book," or "We certainly have noticed some weird images in the illustrations," or "We had better pay close attention to the setting of this section of our historical fiction novel." The use of the first-person plural signals to students that we are in this together, that collectively we will work on making sense of what we are reading.

Consider how different the above sentences would be if you substituted *you* for *we*. The sentences become commands and suggest that teachers have already considered these ideas and their students have somehow failed to do the same. *We* draws our students into a coalition with us as we work together to interpret and understand what we are reading. This sets a better tone for our classroom interactions. It is as if we are "fellow explorers" trying to understand these uncharted textual terrains.

Silent Invitations to Participate

When I am facilitating a discussion, I try to look at other students as well as the student speaking. I do this to signal to other students that I expect them to contribute. When a particular student is offering his or her ideas, I may look at another student and nod and smile to indicate that he or she should consider the talk at hand and prepare to participate. I then redirect my gaze to invite another student to respond next in our discussion. Sometimes by simply walking over and standing next to a student, or looking at him or her when someone else is speaking, we can signal our expectations for participation. Such a subtle, silent invitation does not interrupt our discussion, nor does it require talking on our part. Through our gaze, and physical gestures we can facilitate involvement in our classroom discussions without ever entering into them verbally ourselves.

Wait Time

Another common strategy for eliciting participation is providing wait time for students to consider their ideas and share what they are thinking. However, not all wait time is created equal! Research demonstrates that, on average, teachers wait only a few seconds for a student to offer a response. Since our goal is to encourage thoughtful responses and increased intellectual complexity, we need to give our students time to think about the book at the heart of a discussion and consider their interpretations before we jump in with our response. In the lively world of classroom discussions, our astute silence can be a gift.

Bad Wait Time

We have likely all lived through bad wait time: The whole class stops and stares as a teacher asks a particular student a question, catapulting him or her into an instant hot seat as everyone waits for him or her to respond quickly and correctly.

Good Wait Time

Good wait time is when we allow students time to think and consider what to say while we proceed with the discussion and return to them when they are ready to respond.

In summary, avoid using wait time to call attention to who is paying attention—and who isn't. Wait time should always be used as an invitation for students to accept the gift of a lively discussion.

Try This! ▼ ▼ ▼

For no-fail interactive discussions, it's hard to beat the "turn, pair, and share" strategy. In this simple strategy, we ask students to turn to a partner and share their ideas with one person before asking them to share their ideas with the larger group. This technique allows more voices to be heard and provides support for those students who feel less comfortable sharing in whole-group settings. The goal is to get students talking not just to us, but to one another, whether it be in pairs, in small groups, or with the whole class. This simple strategy is very effective and one of the easiest to implement.

Chart It!

Creating classroom charts that focus students' attention on what has been offered helps us remember what has occurred in previous discussions and fosters more sophisticated discussions. When a discussion is over, there is no record of the discussion outside of our memories unless we purposefully create one. Charts can help bridge the gaps between discussions and help call students' attention to previously discussed concepts. These charts can be the foundation upon which we build subsequent discussions.

I want my students to understand the basic elements and structures of literature and begin using terms such as *plot*, *setting*, *theme*, and *symbolism* throughout our discussions. To support this goal, I create charts in direct proximity to our discussion area that showcase definitions or examples of these terms in my students' own words. Having these charts readily available and using these terms in our discussions by calling students' attention to what they mean in the books we share enables my students to absorb literary terminology into their own vocabularies.

Note This

Allowing students to take notes on what is being read or has been read, to highlight certain sections of a text, or to code the text by placing sticky notes or writing a few words in the book's margin also supports and enhances our discussions. We want to help students prepare to discuss a book, and this doesn't just happen immediately when we finish a text for the first time. Rereading a text and allowing students time to think is a good start, but focusing their ideas through the text by coding or highlighting what is important to them can foster extended discussions.

Sometimes when I am reading a book with younger students, I will keep sticky notes in my lap to serve as "mental placeholders" on a particular page so we may return after completing our read-aloud. I am always balancing the need to move on with the read-aloud and keep the flow of the story going with the students' desire to comment on and discuss the story. Using sticky notes with a word or two written on them can help us keep the story moving while allowing us to return to a particular section for an extended discussion once we've finished reading the book.

Try This! ▼ ▼ ▼

Each of these techniques works in different ways to shape the types of interactions we have with our students. I suggest first trying turn, pair, and share rather than raising hands because this interactive strategy immediately influences the nature of our book discussions. All of these techniques work toward changing the teacher's role from director to facilitator of discussions. The more complicated the technique, the greater the chances that its introduction might interfere with discussions. Start with the simple suggestions and work up to the more complex ones.

Talking Our Hearts Out: Interactive Discussion Strategies

The interactive discussion strategies I am presenting here are not magic. By themselves, they may or may not improve the quality of your classroom interactions. To guarantee successful implementation, these specific suggestions require a supportive, caring classroom environment and a knowledgeable, attentive teacher. The strategies I describe here are the ones I consider most effective in my classrooms, from elementary school to college. They serve as scaffolds for supporting classroom discussions and help expand students' interpretive abilities.

He Said, She Said, I Think

Many students offer their interpretations and ideas without considering the ideas and comments made by students before them. This strategy requires students to state what two other students have offered before sharing their ideas. After discussions have begun, I say to my students, "Okay, now let's try some 'he said, she said, I think.'" Students are then required to restate what two students have said previously, sharing their ideas and interpretations. This strategy accomplishes two important goals. First, it requires students to become active listeners and attend to what other students have said in order to share their ideas. Second, it endorses what other students have said and that those observations can be used as a foundation for subsequent comments. Forcing students to slow down and attend to what other students are saying has positive effects on our classroom discussions.

For example, a student might say, "I noticed that Susan thought the main character was being ridiculous in the way she reacted to the new girl at her school. Then Kathy thought it made sense because she has reacted that way before. But I think that the main character should have discussed the problem with the new girl before she went storming off in the first place." This strategy provides students with an opportunity to agree and disagree politely with other students before offering their own ideas.

First We Thought, Now We Think

In this strategy, adapted from the work of Neil Mercer (1995, 2000), students and the teacher are required to share the changes they have made in their thinking and interpretations. Sharing what we used to think and comparing it to what we are currently thinking can demonstrate our interpretive processes. Teachers can also use it as a summarizing technique to establish credibility about what has been said and how we have reconsidered our positions. By changing our interpretations over the course of a text, we are in effect demonstrating comprehending as a process, not simply an outcome. Our ideas and interpretations do change over time and contexts, and it is important to demonstrate the dynamic nature of the reading and thinking process.

Teachers may use this technique as a summary device, sharing what has been offered up to a particular point and noting the changes in the way the class has been thinking about a book, character, or event. For example, after discussing the opening scenes from a novel, students have particular expectations and predictions for the upcoming events. As a novel continues, we are often surprised by the way the plot changes. Discussing why we thought things were going to happen and how we have changed our minds focuses students' attention on the interpretive process and lets them know it is okay to change your mind and be surprised by the turn of events in a story.

Uptake: Taking Up From What Has Been Offered

This general strategy requires attentive listening on the part of the classroom teacher to use what has been said in subsequent responses and parts of the discussion. Too often, teachers simply provide praise or paraphrase what has been offered rather than substantially commenting on what has been said. *Uptake* is used to clarify and extend what students have said. It is a technique that endorses students' initial responses and interpretations by commenting on their efforts and asking them or other students to take the ideas further. An example may be appropriate here. During a discussion of Katherine Paterson's *Bridge to Terabithia* (1977), a class was discussing the notebook that Jesse kept hidden in his room early in the story.

Ms. R: So, do they have a lot of paper, a lot of supplies, this family?

Andrew: No, not really.

Ms. R: They don't. Okay, so, I'm wondering something . . . If they don't have a lot of money, and here he's got this pad of paper and supplies, do you think it would be a valuable thing or do you think his mom would be mad that he has it?

Sarah: I think it's valuable because he might have spent his money but we don't know, so the mom is probably happy because he doesn't have to go out and buy it.

Ms. R: Okay, so then are you thinking that he's hiding it so that he can protect it and keep it?

Sarah: Protect it from his older sisters because his older sisters went out to buy school supplies when they didn't have any.

Ms. R: And so what might they do if they see he has his, maybe?

Kathy: Steal it.

Ms. R: Okay, and the only reason I'm thinking this is because we've already inferred that the family doesn't have a lot of money, right?

Jonathan: Well, she might be mad that he spent that money but she wouldn't throw it away since then they would be spending even more money to buy it again.

Ms. R: Okay, and again, if we're going to look for proof from the book, is there proof to suggest that Momma would be mad if he spent money?

Talia: Yes, a little bit, because she doesn't want to give it to them.

In this transcript, we can see the teacher taking up from what students have said and asking them to go further in their thinking by asking questions that nudge students to consider their interpretations and ideas. The teacher begins by naming specific contributions from the students, such as how Jesse protected his notebook. She asks the students to return to the book to find evidence supporting their ideas.

This naming of contributions endorses what students say by repeating what has been said and sharing the idea once again in the discussion. What we as teachers repeat and call students' attention to affects what they pay attention to and come to regard as significant. When we say that a student's answer is a good one, other students stop to consider what was good about that comment and how they can offer similar ideas in the future. Our responses have great power in these discussions.

For uptake to be successful, we need extensive knowledge about the book or topic the students are discussing so we know how and when to extend and refine our students' conversational points. In addition, our sensitive listening will enable us to follow what students are saying so we can move from specific contributions to general strategies and instructional suggestions. In this example, Ms. R generalizes from her students' comments how the mother reacted and whether the family is poor and how that affects their behaviors. These gleanings were not stated directly in the text, but she demonstrated how she inferred these ideas from what had occurred in the story.

Platforming: Providing a Foundation During Discussions

From time to time during our discussions, we need to summarize the discussion and remind students what has been said, pull things together, and provide a foundation for the discussion ahead. *Platforming* is a way of putting students' various comments into context, which sets the stage for further discussion by recapping ideas in new language and creating new ways of examining the ideas that emerged through discussion. The idea is to summarize with the goal of moving forward, not backward.

For example, during a discussion about *Where the Wild Things Are*, I said, "Okay, so far we have decided that Max went on an adventure because he was mad at his mother and began treating the Wild Things like his mother treated him. We are also not sure whether he fell asleep or just used his imagination. We also haven't figured out how the supper could still be hot if he was gone more than a year or so. Is there anything else before we move on?"

In this example, I tried to summarize some of the main points my students made with the aim of pulling things together so we could work on fresh thinking in our discussion. So many ideas arise during a good discussion that from time to time teachers need to consolidate and make sense of where the discussion has been. By incorporating some of these summaries on charts, we can also extend our literature discussions across days and rely on our charts to help us remember the conversational ground we have covered.

Three-Part Lists

If you pay close attention to great speeches, political or academic, you will notice from time to time the use of the "three-part list." The three-part list puts together three related points in a row and builds tension for the third point. It is almost like outlining one's points for the audience you are addressing. Three-part lists can make speeches more cohesive and can serve as a form of "verbal outlining" to help the audience understand your points.

Let me provide a quick example. During a speech, I stated, "The problems we have in schools are created by lack of money, lack of time, and lack of support." The emphasis was on the third point, the lack of support. By building up to the last point, we highlight and emphasize it.

Re-Voicing, or Paraphrase Plus

Re-voicing is a way of responding to students that begins by paraphrasing or reformulating students' responses, adding to what has been said and allowing students to speak back to what they originally mentioned. Mary Catherine O'Connor and Sarah Michaels (1993) have detailed the process of re-voicing, and I will simply share briefly how it works in classroom discussions. A teacher begins by saying, "So, I am hearing you say . . ." This is called an "inference marker." In other words, we link to what a student has offered and then paraphrase what has been said. We continue, ". . . that you think Max was behaving like his mother in *Where the Wild Things Are*." In this technique we restate what our student has offered, and then end with "Is that what you meant?" This final question allows the student to end the conversational turn by adding to what he or she said previously, and to reject the paraphrase or confirm it.

This way of returning the discussion to the students and inviting them to address their comments is an important strategy. Too often, we unintentionally end the conversational turn by evaluating what has been said (the *E* in IRE—instruct, respond, evaluate). In this way, we always seem to get in the last word. Re-voicing provides a way to allow students the last word and endorses their contributions. When we restate what students have said, we can move from specifics to generalities, build metaphors to help students make connections, reconsider what has been offered, and validate students' ideas. This alone can dramatically change the interaction patterns in our classrooms.

Finding Books Worth Talking About

Finally, as we consider how to improve the quality of our discussions, let's make sure we're reading something worth discussing. We need to be sure that what we select to read with our students is literature that is relevant to their lives and worth talking about. I try hard to select books that contain a depth of meaning so we can dig deep and revisit the text again and again. Sometimes, when our discussions fall flat, it may simply be that the book we chose didn't yield the material needed for a rich discussion.

Sometimes, teachers of younger students report that their students don't have anything of consequence to say when they finish reading aloud. First I ask whether they have talked about their expectations for discussions with students. Then I ask them what book they read. As much as I love Bill Martin's *Brown Bear, Brown Bear, What Do You See?* (1992) and understand its role in primary-grade classrooms, it is not going to initiate or sustain quality in-depth discussions. If we want meaty discussions, we have to read books with some meat on their textual bones.

Try This! ▾ ▾ ▾

Make a list of the books you have read this year and mark those that have supported the best discussions. Compare the characteristics of the books that sparked lively discussions with those that fell short of expectations. Use these characteristics as a guide for future book selections. Books that spark great discussions generally have:

1. Quality writing

2. Relevance to the students' lives

3. Accessible topics, writing, and text structures

4. Perspectives that are not didactic

5. Gradual revelation of all levels of the story

Conclusion

One of the challenges of facilitating great discussions is learning how to offer your ideas without dominating what is being said and thought. As teachers, we have a very powerful position in our classrooms. What we say typically carries more weight than anyone else's comments or opinions. Because of this, we need to be cautious about how we offer our opinions. Sometimes we need to sneak our ideas through the side door, rather than barging through the front door telling everyone what they should be thinking.

Chained utterances are a good indicator that we are not dominating the discussion and controlling the floor. Chained utterances are occurrences when students are speaking one after another without the teacher intervening between every comment. Instead of the traditional IRE pattern, it is more like an I-RRRR pattern; in other words, extending from our initial comment, students are allowed and supported to continue the discussion with one another as well as with us. When we make comments after every student statement, we tend to dominate the direction of the discussion and end up losing sight of students' ideas.

Douglas Barnes (1992) makes the astute observation that discussions should make "invisible children visible." In many classrooms and discussions, some children tend to move to the periphery. Some feel they have nothing to say; others are uncomfortable saying what they think. We need to develop a safe, supportive environment where students know they are welcome to say what they think without fear of reprisal and to develop what Martin Nystrand (1997) calls an "ethos of involvement." We want everyone involved in the life of our classrooms, especially in our discussions. We want children to feel capable of articulating their ideas, to welcome vigorous debate (even if it means their ideas are challenged), and, in the process, to gain new insights and consider new meanings.

Great discussions generate energy. It is the same energy that comedians and actors are drawn to in improvisation. When we're swept up in an invigorating discussion, we're able to fly without a script; what's more, we don't need to worry about landing on a predetermined spot. The energy comes from the excitement of not knowing what anyone will say next or where the next interpretation may take us. This is the stuff that makes for great teaching and great discussions—and forms the core of reading comprehension.

CHAPTER 4

ASKING QUESTIONS

Providing Space for
Student Response

Asking more open-ended questions will not
change the quality of children's thinking if they
continue to think there is only one correct answer.
—*Debra Myhill (2006)*

Teachers ask lots of questions. Asking questions is an "instructional move"—one
of the things we teachers do during our discussions. Unfortunately, we often overrely on asking questions, in particular literal questions, as our primary instructional
move. We ask questions to stimulate discussions, check on students' comprehension
of what has been read, clarify and extend students' responses, manage interactions,
and call students' attention to particular aspects of the texts we are discussing.

Research has demonstrated time and again that teachers ask too many questions and, in the process, dominate classroom interactions and spend too much time on literal aspects of texts. In addition, we often use questions as our primary classroom management technique. The types of questions we ask, the manner in which they're posed, and their effects on students' thinking and responses are some of the most important aspects of classroom talk and demand our attention.

Three assumptions underlie the types of questions we ask and our reasons for asking them.

1. Certain meanings are more important than others, and the teacher believes he or she knows which of these meanings is correct. Often, teachers ask questions to provide students with an opportunity to offer the interpretations teachers have already decided are correct. Teachers believe they have privileged access to a book's meaning and ask questions to see whether their students can provide answers that align with their thinking. When we do this, what we are really asking students is "Guess what's in my head?"

2. In general, most of the questions teachers ask can be answered by referring directly to the text. The research I have conducted and the reviews of research available in the professional literature suggest that teachers favor asking literal questions. These questions privilege the text over the thinking of the reader by locating the answers directly on the page. These questions simply expect students to remember what was in the book and regurgitate it during discussions. Its focus is on students' memory, not their thinking.

3. Teachers believe that the best way to assess students' knowledge and understandings is through questioning. They ask questions to know whether students have comprehended what has been read. Although it's possible to assess comprehension this way, we often overrely on such questioning.

Listening to the ideas students offer freely, considering the questions students ask, and allowing students to represent and articulate their understandings in a variety of ways will help us overcome our focus on questions, especially literal ones, as our primary source of information. If we don't unpack and rethink these assumptions, they will continue to limit the effectiveness of the questions we ask in our instructional practices and classroom discussions. What impact do these questions have on our students?

First, students' answers often reflect the questions we ask. In other words, if we want students to think in more complex and sophisticated ways, we need to ask more complex and sophisticated questions. It should be self-evident that when we ask literal questions we get literal answers. These literal questions send a potent message to our students about what aspects of the text we think are most important. However, as stated in the opening epigraph, simply asking more complex questions without setting different expectations for our students' responses is insufficient to ensure more complex thinking. We need to be sure that students realize the questions we ask have integrity, meaning they are questions we don't know the answers to. We need to make sure that students know we actually want to hear what they honestly think. Maybe an example would help us understand what I am suggesting. Here is a discussion centering on the picture book *The Three Pigs* by David Wiesner (2001). Pay close attention to the questions the teacher asked and how they affected the responses students offered.

Ms. H: What did you say, Juan?

Juan: That one of the pigs was shaking and another pig said, "That's enough."

Ms. H: The pig was shaking what?

Juan: The picture.

Ms. H: Good! He was shaking the page, and then what was happening when he was shaking the page?

Juan: The letters were falling?

Ms. H: The letters were falling. Okay, and as the letters were falling, what was happening, Jennifer?

Jennifer: The dragon was catching them in a basket.

Ms. H: The dragon was putting them in a basket. What else did you notice as the letters were going into the basket?

Jeffrey: Maybe the dragon in the story stole the letters.

Ms. H: That was something that was said the other day. I will write it down on our chart. The horns from the dragon knocked some of the letters down, which was a good observation. But I kind of want to go back. What else happened when the dragon put them in the basket? One other thing happened. I said what happened a few times going around to the tables during our small group discussions. What does that page say?

Emily: That's enough.

Ms. H: Right! He says, "That's enough." Good!

Clearly, the teacher in this transcript had a particular idea in mind and asked questions until students offered or displayed what she wanted to hear. I would suggest that these types of questions have little integrity, meaning they are not authentic—the teacher asked questions she already knew the answers to and expected her students to simply guess what was in her head or on the page. I believe that too often the discussions we have in classrooms are similar to the one displayed above. Focusing solely on the literal elements of a text changes the nature and the tenor of our discussions, privileging the elements in the text over the ideas, values, experiences, and interpretations that readers bring to the text.

Throughout this exchange, the classroom teacher had opportunities to ask her students about their responses, but never ventured down that road. She never asked her students what they were thinking, but merely considered each response and determined whether it was the one she was looking for. I will address recognizing and taking advantage of these opportunities, or what I call "critical junctures," in Chapter 6.

Second, students may see the questions we ask as confrontational rather than invitational. I have observed classrooms where children seem anxious to be called on, and when asked a question they seem to shut down or simply guess what they think the teacher wants to hear. The questions we ask should invite students to articulate their understandings for other students to consider. Questions should serve as invitations to discuss and ponder, not as challenges to fear.

Third, it is unfortunate, but research has suggested that questions are often used to control students' behavior rather than support inquiry. When teachers call on students they believe are not paying attention, they are using questions to manage the interactions, not to delve into students' thinking. I never understood why teachers seem to wait until you are not paying attention to call on you. I used to sit in classrooms daydreaming, knowing that as soon as I wandered away in my head I would get called on. I often wondered why the teacher didn't call on me when I was obviously engaged in the discussion at hand.

Finally, who gets to ask the majority of the questions reflects who is in control of the ideas and thinking in the classroom. In study after study, from the work of John Goodlad (1984), published in *A Place Called School*, to the classic research conducted by Dolores Durkin, and continuing more recently with the work of Michael Pressley and others, researchers have demonstrated time and again that teachers ask 80 to 90 percent of the questions during the average school day. This rarely allows time for students to pose questions because they are too busy answering ours. It seems that teachers ask questions to keep control of the discussions, rather than to investigate what students are thinking. This doesn't mean that a few well-placed questions aren't effective discussion tools, it just means that we ask too many. Maybe that's why we are so tired by day's end.

Try This! ▼ ▼ ▼

Let a student act as the teacher and lead a discussion. Pay close attention to what the student does. The questions the student asks and the ways in which he or she talks with other students may reveal a great deal about the way you interact with your students. It can be quite revealing to see ourselves through the ways in which our students imitate us.

Four Types of Questions

Most of the research about questions and questioning techniques organizes the types of questions teachers ask into four general categories.

1. *Display questions* require students to recall information that is embedded in the literal text and "display" their knowledge through their answers.

2. *Procedural questions* address the way things operate in the classroom and the procedures that govern classroom life, especially the expectations for classroom discussions.

3. *Process questions* are directed at how a student arrived at a particular answer or interpretation. In other words, these require students to discuss their thinking processes and how they make sense of their literary experiences.

4. *Inquiry questions* are directed at students' interpretations. They are honest questions, investigating why students think the way they do. They are often referred to as "open-ended" or "higher-order" questions.

Display Questions

Display or literal questions serve as cues to narrow students' answers to align to what is predetermined as correct by the teacher or the teaching manual. They are inauthentic questions, meaning they do not regularly occur in conversations outside of school settings. These literal questions privilege the knowledge of the teacher or what is displayed in the text itself over the knowledge of the reader. They are "pseudo" questions, often resulting in what I like to call "oral fill-in-the-blank" discussions. In some ways, answering literal questions is a matter of simply stating the obvious. The literal text is there for all to see, so why should we continue to ask questions about what has already been said?

Display questions develop passive students. These questions focus on the literal text, limit the range of acceptable answers to one correct response, promote reaching agreement and consensus, and are often accompanied by choral responses. Here are some examples of display questions:

- ▲ What is the main idea of the story?

- ▲ What happened in the beginning of the story?

- ▲ Where did the character go at the end of the story?

- ▲ What is the setting of the story?

- ▲ Whose picture was on the cover of the book?

Although I firmly believe that we tend to ask too many literal questions, occasionally such questions may be appropriate. For example, when a teacher wants to review or emphasize a point, calling students' attention to something that was stated in the text, display questions may be appropriate to ask. These questions can establish common understandings among members of the class and help to consolidate or summarize information previously encountered in the text. When reading a chapter book aloud across a number of days, we often begin by asking students what happened the previous day before we begin reading the next chapter. Even if we remember where we are in the story, we want to be sure that all of our students remember as well, so we use display questions to recap where we have been in the book. These questions get ideas into a "public space" so they may be considered and reconsidered by our students.

It is not my contention that literal questions should never be used, but I would suggest that they not represent 80 to 90 percent of the questions we ask. I want students to see the literal text as a "point of departure"—where our discussions begin—not the focus of our entire discussion.

Procedural Questions

Procedural questions remind students of the established procedures and expectations in our classrooms. Asking these questions can help facilitate our discussions and provide support for students' behaviors. Asking students what they are expected to do next can remind them of how discussions work in our classrooms and how students are expected to answer and behave. Here are some examples:

- ▲ When we are discussing a text, what helps us listen to one another?
- ▲ When the teacher is reading a book aloud, what do we do with the Post-its on our clipboards, and how do we share ideas?
- ▲ How do we gain access to the discussion?
- ▲ Where do we sit when we are reading and discussing a text?
- ▲ How are we supposed to write in our response logs after we read?

We call students' attention to the procedures and expectations in our classrooms by asking them to restate the expectations and class rules we have previously constructed with them. These can be very effective in maintaining the quality of our discussions, but should be used sparingly as students become more and more accustomed to our classroom procedures. They are simply a technique for reminding students of what we expect them to do and how to do it.

Process Questions

We use process questions to understand students' interpretive moves or thought processes. These questions focus our attention on how we make sense of texts, not the specific sense we make. Asking *what* leads students to offer facts; asking *why* prompts them to discuss their interpretations and how they arrived at them. Process questions address students' metacognitive processes and require them to turn their attention inward to focus on how they generate interpretations. They serve as a map of our "thought journeys." Here are some examples:

▲ What connections, insights, and comparisons did you make as you were reading the text?

▲ How did you generate your ideas?

▲ What did you notice in the illustrations that led you to make that assumption?

▲ What ideas, comments, or evidence from the text influenced your thinking?

▲ What went on in your thinking as I read the last chapter of our book?

We want to know how students are making sense of what they read to provide support and help them manage the challenges offered by the texts they experience. These questions serve as a foundation for the comprehension strategies that we teach.

Try This! ▼ ▼ ▼

Record a literature discussion focusing on a familiar picture book. Listen to the recording, count the number of questions asked, and organize the questions into the following two categories: literal questions (focusing on the text) and inferential questions (centered on students' thinking and inferences). Did you ask too many literal questions? How did students respond differently, depending on the types of questions that were asked? Did the questions you asked lead students to respond in ways you were hoping they would? Consider the implications of the types of questions you asked.

In a setting outside of a school classroom—at the dinner table at your own home, for example, or at an informal gathering—ask questions that you already know the answers to. Pay attention to how people react to this type of questioning. Ask yourself why we ask our students these inauthentic questions. Does this type of question help students reveal what they are thinking?

Inquiry Questions

Inquiry questions are honest questions that allow for an acceptable range of answers. These questions are concerned with possibilities, not necessarily with literal correctness. Like process questions, they view the literal text as a point of departure, the place where interpretations begin. They acknowledge the multiple perspectives, interpretations, and understandings that students construct as they read, and allow them to move beyond literal recall to more sophisticated interpretations.

The importance of inquiry questions cannot be overstated; sadly, we rarely invite our students to consider inquiry questions. Here are some examples from my own classroom discussions:

▲ What are your initial impressions of the text?

▲ What caught your attention? What did you notice?

▲ What seemed unique or peculiar?

▲ How does this connect with what you know?

▲ What other meanings are possible?

▲ Have you considered other students' ideas?

▲ How do alternative interpretations affect your ideas?

▲ What do these ideas mean for your future reading?

▲ Are any of the characters privileged or marginalized?

▲ What attitudes or worldviews are endorsed or diminished?

▲ What assumptions are taken for granted?

▲ How are critical issues (race, gender, class, ethnicity) dealt with?

Inquiry questions can be challenging questions to ask and answer. The problem may be that we have asked so many literal questions in school that students just aren't prepared to answer questions that make them think. Inquiry questions require students to think beyond the text, to infer from their experiences and understandings, to consider the author's intentions, and to construct and articulate more sophisticated understandings. Inquiry questions lie at the heart of quality classroom discussions.

Try This! ▼ ▼ ▼

Have students preview selected picture books in small groups and create a list of questions to ask other students that they think will generate an engaging discussion. These lists reveal the types of questions students think are important and can be used to extend discussions. Students often ask questions that we would not consider. This strategy enlivens our discussions and encourages student participation.

Closing Remarks

In my book *Reading Aloud and Beyond: Fostering the Intellectual Life with Older Readers* (Serafini & Giorgis, 2003), I offered some considerations for the types of questions we ask and how we ask them. I include them here, and have added a few more to serve as a summary on the role of questions in our classroom discussions.

Considerations for Asking Questions

Questions should:

1. Provide space for an acceptable range of answers, possibilities, and interpretations.

2. Help readers make connections or discuss disconnections to their lives and other literary experiences.

3. Promote further inquiry, discussion, and reflection, allowing students to extend, clarify, and confirm their interpretations.

4. Be responsive—that is, asked in response to a student's ideas as way to extend a student's line of thinking.

5. Be on target and streamlined; asking too many questions, even good ones, can shut down a good discussion.

6. Have integrity; teachers should avoid asking questions meant to simply check up on or control students—when teachers already know the answers to the questions they ask, the questions lose their authenticity.

7. Help students explain or justify their ideas.

8. Scaffold students' learning.

9. Help students notice things in the text they may not have noticed on their own; questions should address what is in the text as well as students' interpretations of text.

10. Go beyond literal recall and ask students to provide evidence of their interpretive processes.

11. Encourage students to ask more questions.

12. Nudge students to talk about their thinking; "What are you thinking?" may be a better way to get to their interpretive processes than asking "why" questions.

The pressures to cover the required curriculum may be the driving force in our tendency to default to literal and display questions. Teachers may ask, "With so much material to get through, how can we allow our students to wander and wonder?" I understand this pressure, and have felt it myself in both my elementary- and college-level teaching. However, we are teaching children to think, not simply memorize facts. The questions we ask and the answers we expect should demonstrate the thinking and talk that we value and help students develop more sophisticated ways of thinking and interpreting the literature they encounter.

CHAPTER 5

LITERACY DEMONSTRATIONS
The Language of Explicit Instruction

In other words, it is true that we are often less explicit than we might be, that we are confusing sometimes when we try to be explicit, and being more thoughtfully explicit can be important.

—*Peter Johnston (2004)*

The word *teach* comes from the Greek and Latin words that mean "to show." The etymology of *teach* has important implications for how we approach comprehension instruction. When we teach students to read and comprehend, we are actually *demonstrating* how a proficient reader reads and comprehends a text. In fact, most reading instruction is based on demonstrating the various strategies that proficient readers use to comprehend texts. The challenge lies in the fact that the strategies or cognitive "operations" that proficient readers employ to make sense of texts are basically invisible, meaning that we can't observe someone summarizing or visualizing. To demonstrate these comprehension strategies, we need to use language to explain to our students what is going on in our heads as we read and make sense of texts.

One of the most important distinctions between the language used during literature discussions and the language employed in comprehension lessons is the focus and explicitness of the language. In comprehension lessons, teachers use language to call students' attention to particular aspects of reading and literature, have specific objectives for the lesson, choose language and resources to support this focus, and confirm students' responses that are connected to the objective of the lesson. The language used in comprehension lessons is *explanatory*, not *exploratory*, like the language used during our literature discussions. During our comprehension lessons, we have specific directions and goals for our lessons, and we use language to focus students' attention on these goals.

What Makes Language and Instruction Explicit?

In some ways, our literature discussions are times when we talk *with* students, and our comprehension lessons are when we talk *to* students. The challenge is learning what constitutes supportive, explicit language and what constitutes language that may be confusing or redundant. In my book *Lessons in Comprehension: Explicit Instruction in the Reading Workshop* (Serafini, 2004), I described explicit instruction in this manner:

Explicit instruction is often considered the opposite of vague, implicit, or embedded instruction. The word *explicit*, when attached to the word *instruction*, implies a more sequential, more rigorous type of instruction when compared to the embedded instruction often associated with workshop approaches to reading comprehension instruction. Simply adhering to a series of instructional moves does not guarantee that explicit instruction has taken place. The degree of "explicitness" in an instructional experience hinges upon the language used in the instructional event and the relationship that is developed between the teacher and students during the instructional transaction. What may be very explicit to one student may be quite vague to another. (p. 5)

This definition implies that explicitness is not simply a characteristic of language itself, but is developed in specific contexts between the one explaining something (the teacher) and the one learning something (the student). In addition, some important aspects of the language used during explicit comprehension instruction are as follows.

1. *Remains Focused.* The language used in comprehension lessons calls students' attention to particular aspects of a text or reading strategy to focus their attention on what is being presented. The language we use during our comprehension lessons supports our instructional objectives and intentions.

2. *Relates to previous experiences.* We use terms that are familiar to our students, drawing on our shared experiences to help our students understand new ideas and concepts. One of the primary advantages that classroom teachers have over the authors of scripted programs is that they understand what their

students have experienced previously and can draw on this information to make connections during their lessons.

3. *Allows for approximations.* While the lesson objectives that teachers create may be focused and predetermined, students need time and support to learn new ideas and strategies. The language that we employ invites students to consider what has been offered and allows them to come to understand what is being taught.

4. *Limits the degree of difficulty.* The language that teachers use during an explicit comprehension lesson limits the challenges that students have with the new material. Language serves as the primary scaffold, reducing the difficulty of a task by breaking it down into manageable parts and offering multiple ways to consider the things being taught.

5. *Sustains engagement.* The best lessons are those that promote and sustain student engagement in what is being taught. The language that we use should encourage students to engage in the task at hand and continue to do so after the lesson is over. The quality of our reading lessons is judged by what students are able to do *after* the lesson is over.

6. *Focuses on appropriate pacing.* In our school system, the amount of time we have to conduct lessons and teach reading each day is limited. Because of this, the language we use has to help move the lesson along. The appropriate pace for a lesson depends on the complexity of what is being taught and the understandings of the students participating in the lesson. A good lesson isn't so slow as to be boring, nor so fast that it is confusing.

Try This! ▾ ▾ ▾

Record a comprehension lesson and compare the language used with the language you used in your literature discussion. Consider the following questions:

1. How did you begin the lesson? Did you state what your objectives were?

2. Were the questions you asked more specific?

3. How did you keep the lesson moving?

4. How did you respond to students' efforts?

5. How did you use language to explain particular concepts, ideas, or strategies? How did you use language to be explicit?

The language of instruction is expository, meaning it is used to explain things and to provide information for novice readers. I mentioned earlier that language is the primary scaffold teachers use to help readers do things they could not do on their own. I would like to expand on that comment briefly here. Scaffolds are temporary devices used to help builders and architects create structures. In much the same way, scaffolds in teaching are structures that provide temporary support for learners. We use language to help readers make sense of what they are reading by focusing their attention on specific aspects of a text or the reading process, to avoid failure by ensuring a manageable degree of difficulty in a task, and to employ reading strategies they would not be able to use on their own.

It is through language that we bring the cognitive aspects of reading together with its social aspects. We use language to demonstrate what has been going on in our heads and to think aloud about how we make sense of texts. In other words, it is through language that we make the invisible process of comprehension visible.

Try This! ▼ ▼ ▼

Explain something—any topic or idea—to a colleague and pay attention to the language you use and references you draw upon to make something understood. When we are explaining something, we tend to draw upon common understandings to explain new ideas. We often use metaphors to make comparisons between what is known and what is not known. Consider the implications of this for your teaching. How do we help students make sense of new ideas if we can't connect these ideas to things they already understand? How can we use metaphors and comparisons effectively to help students understand new concepts and strategies?

Think-Alouds

This chapter will focus on the language we employ when we think aloud in front of our students to make our comprehension processes visible. In general, think-alouds can focus on three important aspects of reading comprehension. For each of these three aspects of comprehension, I provide an example of a think-aloud that addresses these concepts:

1. Navigating and noticing textual and visual elements

2. Interpreting text and images

3. Extending interpretations beyond the text

Navigating and Noticing Textual and Visual Elements

Let's begin with a think-aloud focusing on navigating and noticing textual and visual elements of a book, in particular a children's picture book. By thinking aloud in front of my students and using language they are familiar with and references they have experienced, I am able to show how I approach a picture book, what I attend to, and how I begin to interpret what I am reading. The purpose of this think-aloud is to get students to pay attention to important elements in the book and activate the prior knowledge necessary to comprehend the story.

> Good morning, readers! This morning, I am going to do what is called a "think-aloud" with the book *Wolf!* [Bloom, 1999] to give you an idea of what goes on in my head when I pick up a book. I like to take time when I first encounter a new picture book to consider what is on the cover, the title page, the end pages, and all the other stuff that is included in the book before the story begins. I think doing this helps me get ready to understand the book better.
>
> When I approach this book, the first thing I think of when I see the title, *Wolf!*, is the wolf in *The Three Little Pigs*. Maybe it's because there is a pig in the illustration on the cover. Immediately, when I hear the word *wolf* I think of certain things because I have read a lot of stories—mostly fairy tales—where there's a wolf in the story. So when I see a children's picture book like this with the title *Wolf!*, I'm thinking to myself, "big, bad wolf." I'm also noticing in the illustration that this wolf and the cow are wearing glasses. The wolf is reading a book. The first thing I think to myself is that these aren't real wolves or real cows because I've never seen a cow wearing glasses or a wolf wearing glasses or reading a book. So I know it's an imaginary story, you know, a fictional story.

I also like to take a close look at the end pages because I always think there are clues about the story in the end pages. I noticed in the end pages there is a wolf carrying a bandanna, kind of like the old hobos used to do when they wandered through a town. Everyone is kind of looking at the wolf as he walks by. I'm thinking to myself, "Maybe this story is about a wolf coming into a new town or going somewhere new." I don't know what this has to do with the wolf yet, but I think it may be important. Then I notice on the back cover there are two rabbits reading a book. I ask myself, "Where do the rabbits come into the story?" So as I approach a new book I am asking myself questions and thinking about what I have noticed so far.

Now I'm going to look at the cover page. It says it is written by Becky Bloom and illustrated by Pascal Biet. I've never read a book by Becky Bloom before, so I have no idea what to expect. I've never seen illustrations by Pascal Biet, but they look kind of like watercolors. The characters are depicted as friendly, fictional animals and don't look too scary. On the title page, I notice that the wolf is writing letters across a piece of paper: *A-A-A-A*, then *B-B-B-B*. I remember back in elementary school I used to have to do that, and I hated it. It seems that the book has something to do with writing and school. I wonder if the wolf is going to go to school. I'm just about ready to start reading the book now, so let's talk about what I did.

At this point in the lesson, I would review with my students what they noticed me doing during the think-aloud lesson, and we might make a chart to support how we approach a fictional picture book. For me, this is an important lesson, and one that I would demonstrate early in the year. The lesson focuses on how I navigate and identify the elements of a book. I would have students take some picture books that I make available and try approaching a picture book in the same manner, using the same strategies that I've just demonstrated.

Interpreting Text and Images

The most important aspect of reading is making sense of or interpreting what we read. It is the primary objective of any encounter with a text or image. One of our most important instructional objectives as reading teachers is to ensure that students understand comprehension is the ultimate goal of reading. I certainly want students to notice important elements in a book and to be able to decode the text and navigate its structures, but most important, I want them to use these skills to make sense of what they read. During a think-aloud on interpreting texts, I share with my students how I make sense of what I read by connecting to other texts, my own experiences, and the world itself. Interpretation is a process of sense-making, drawing on a variety of resources to do so. My think-aloud will provide students with insights into how I do that.

Good morning, readers! Today we are going to read and make sense of an interesting picture book by Anthony Browne entitled *Piggybook* [1986]. As I have demonstrated before, we will pay close attention to the visual and textual elements of the book, especially the cover, end pages, and title page, before we read the story. But today's think-aloud will focus on how I make sense of the story as I read through it. I want to share with you how I comprehend what I am reading. We all know that comprehending is our primary goal when we read. It is what successful readers do, correct? Okay, let me show you how I do it, and then we will talk about things you notice and some ideas to help you make sense of what you are reading.

To begin, after reviewing the cover, the end pages and the title page, I am pretty sure that this book is going to be about the challenges between men and women, or boys and girls, and how they get along. I know this because the mom is carrying the whole family on her back in the illustration on the cover, and the blurb on the back cover gives me some clues as to where the book is headed. What I am not sure of yet is why the hand on the back cover looks like a pig's hoof. Maybe it is a reference to the term "male chauvinist pig." This term refers to men who treat women unfairly and talk like men are far superior to women. Historically, men have held most of the power in the world. Whether we like that or not, it is the way things have been. I wonder just how much Anthony Browne will bring this idea into his story.

As I begin reading the book, I notice that the male members of the family are always drawn in bright colors, whereas the mother is shaded in dull brown illustrations. I think this might have something to do with how she is treated and may relate to what Browne is trying to say in the theme of this book. Next, I notice how the boys and the father talk to the mother. Let me tell you something—if I ever talked to my mother like that, or my father called for his meal by saying, "Hurry up, old girl," we would have gone hungry every night. It bothers me how the mother is treated in the story, but I think that is what Browne wants.

As I continue to read, I am not surprised that the mother just leaves; what I am surprised by is how Browne turns the male characters into actual pigs. Pigs start showing up everywhere in the illustrations. Some are obvious and some are hidden. Browne is illustrating the transformation of the characters into pigs by using symbols throughout his illustrations. Remember when we talked about symbols and logos and how they are used to represent things? Browne seems to be doing this quite a bit.

Just when the men are about to really hit rock bottom, scrounging around on the floor for food, the mother comes home. In the illustration, she is positioned above the men, showing the power she now has over them, while they grovel at her feet. This is a real change in the story. Suddenly, the boys and the father start doing household chores and treating the mom better. Wow, that was pretty fast. The men really learned their lesson quickly. I don't think in real life people change that quickly, but it is interesting that Browne did this in the story. The real surprise in the story is when the mom ends up fixing the car at the end. I didn't expect that. I also noticed that the license plate on the car is *123 PIGS*, spelled backward. That seems to connect to all the fairy tales I have read.

It seems to me that this book is all about how men and women treat each other, and what happens when you try to take advantage of someone and treat them with disrespect. I really enjoy looking closely at Browne's illustrations because he puts so many details in them that you have to pay attention to. I want to go back and look at some of the artwork that he uses on the walls in the house. I think they refer to famous paintings, and I want to know what the actual paintings are. These may be more symbols that I missed the first time through. Do you have any questions about what I did? What might you have done while reading this book?

In this think-aloud, I demonstrated how I would actually approach and interpret a picture book. My goal was to offer readers insights into how I make sense of texts, what questions I ask as I read, and what connections I make to other stories and my own experiences. I try to keep the interpretations I share with my students tentative. It is important to explain that there are numerous possibilities in every text and illustration, and that your interpretations are not the only ones possible.

Extending Interpretations Beyond the Text

Taking what is presented in a text and extending the ideas beyond the pages of the book into the realities and experiences in the world is an important aspect of reading comprehension. We make sense of every text and experience based on all the other texts we have read and experiences we have lived through. Making connections between our lives and the texts we encounter is the primary way we understand what we read. In this sense, reading comprehension always extends beyond the covers of the book being read.

In this think-aloud, I will demonstrate how I connect a picture book with current events, other texts, music lyrics, poetry, and other visual images. My connections are based on my extensive knowledge of the world. I would not expect students to make the same connections; however, I know they will connect the picture book with their own experiences, which are different from my own.

Good morning, readers! Today we are going to talk about connecting what we read with what we know and have experienced in our own lives. Each book we read reminds us of things we have seen, heard, read, and experienced. This means that we have to look in the book and in the world to make sense of what we are reading. The book I have selected to do a think-aloud with today is called *Sister Anne's Hands* by Marybeth Lorbiecki [1998]. As always, before I read the book, I consider the title, cover, end pages, and title page information. The cover illustration shows a small girl and a nun. When I was young I went to church and took classes taught by nuns. Some of them were really nice, but others were pretty mean. When I look at the cover of this book, it looks like this nun might be really nice. I am going to read through the book first, and then we are going to talk about the ideas in the story before I introduce some other things to you.

As you just heard, this book is about prejudice, especially toward African Americans. I want you to listen to a song by the band U2 called "Pride (In the Name of Love)." I have printed up the words to the song so we can read them as we listen. When we are finished, we are going to read a poem by Langston Hughes called "I, Too." I think as we read and listen to these three different texts we are going to see some connections among the ideas presented.

The first connection that I make is about being proud of who you are, regardless of your color, race, gender, or where you come from. For me, this is an important theme in all three of these texts. The second thing that connects for me is how ashamed people should be if they don't realize how narrow-minded they are when they don't respect other people and can't see past the color of their skin.

The last text I want to share is a famous quote from Martin Luther King, Jr., In this quote he stated, "I have a dream that my four little children will one day live in a nation where they will not be judged by the color of their skin but by the content of their character." Let's talk a bit about how this quote builds upon the discussion we are having about the other texts.

In this think-aloud, I have demonstrated how texts are connected and how bringing together more than one text or image about a topic can expand our understandings and lead to new insights. I am always looking for songs and poems that connect to the picture books and novels that we read in our class. There are numerous ways to connect texts: across themes, genres, topics, formats, authors, or illustrators. Each connection provides different ways of comprehending each individual text. By bringing other texts and the experiences of our lives into our discussions, we expand what it means to comprehend.

Closing Comments

The language and think-alouds demonstrated in this chapter are designed to provide you with possible lessons for helping young readers see what successful readers do when they are reading. These demonstrations are used to get students to engage with texts and come to know how proficient readers comprehend what they read. Novice readers need to see what successful readers do, to see themselves as capable of employing the same strategies, and to see the many purposes in what is being demonstrated.

I mentioned that I share my interpretations tentatively. I want students to see my puzzlements as well as my certainties. I believe it is important to demonstrate that comprehension is not a narrow concept, that many viable meanings can be constructed during the reading of a text. What I want to demonstrate is not necessarily the *products* of reading a text—the meanings constructed—but the *process* of making sense. My think-alouds are designed to help students understand how I make sense, not just the sense I make.

CHAPTER 6

CRITICAL JUNCTURES
Exploring the Possibilities of Response

Two roads diverged in a wood, and I—
I took the one less traveled by,
And that has made all the difference.

—*Robert Frost*

Spending time as a researcher in various elementary classrooms, I have noticed, in my position as an observer without the responsibility of teaching, when students offer ideas that seem to go beyond what was expected, posing "interpretive possibilities" during a discussion. These students are providing opportunities for expanding the discussion in new and interesting directions. Some educators have referred to these incidents as "teachable moments" because they offer possibilities for teaching. However, teachers must first choose from a variety of ways to proceed. Because of this, I have chosen to call these teachable moments "critical junctures."

To be sure, it is easier to recognize critical junctures when I am sitting in the back of the classroom taking notes or when I retreat to my office to examine the transcripts from a class's discussions. It is much harder to attend to the possibilities that arise during a discussion when we are "in the foam" of teaching. However, this is the essence of effective teaching. To be able to realize the potential in what students offer demands that we go into our discussions well prepared, ready to recognize when these possibilities arise. Lately, I have been asking myself, "How do we recognize when these critical junctures take place? How do we decide on their instructional or interpretive merit or potential? And subsequently, how do we take advantage of these teachable moments?"

Courtney Cazden (1986) has recommended that we "heighten our awareness of possibility" in our teaching and discussions. A heightened awareness requires us to fully understand the content of the book we are discussing, become sensitive to the comments and interpretations offered by our students, know how to facilitate a discussion to expand the possibilities of our encounters, and evaluate the merit or potential of the interpretations our students offer. My friend Erin Murphy, a fellow educator, said that the responses that offer the most opportunities are "little comments with big possibilities."

To take full advantage of these teachable moments during our literature discussions, we need to recognize that we face numerous decisions about the best way to proceed at any moment in the discussion. If we are following a script, or if we ask questions with only one predetermined correct answer, we would eliminate the possibilities of these critical junctures because there is only one path to follow. Let us begin by recognizing when these critical junctures occur and take advantage of the possibilities they offer.

Interactive Comprehension Strategies: Fostering Meaningful Talk About Text

Taking the Road Less Traveled

A juncture, like the junctions we encounter while driving our cars, provides us with choices of ways to proceed. We recognize them from our car because of the characteristics of the road itself; the junctures are not as evident in our teaching and classroom discussions. Our ability to recognize critical junctures begins with our ability to carefully and sensitively listen to what students are saying. However, what students are saying is only relevant in relationship to the possibilities and meanings provided by the texts we are reading and discussing. Our ability to listen closely and carefully and really hear what students are saying is predicated on the knowledge base we bring to the lessons and discussions in our classrooms. We do best in this capacity when we can draw from an extensive knowledge of children's and young adult literature, literary theories, reading processes, and classroom interactions to enhance students' interpretive repertoires. In other words, many of these critical junctures will go unnoticed if we don't have the requisite knowledge to recognize their potential.

One of the primary considerations in recognizing what to do during a discussion is to look for comments and interpretations that move the discussion beyond the literal text into interpretation and analysis. When students simply refer to the literal text, there may be limited potential in their comments, and therefore limited opportunities to extend the discussion. The focus of these literal responses is always back on the written text or images contained in a book themselves. We must consider what our students have noticed, what they have overlooked, why they noticed something, and whether these things are important; however, we also need to be alert for times when students move beyond the noticing and naming of literal elements in the text to making interpretations and offering analyses. One cue that this may be happening is when students use the word *because* in their responses. This word often serves as an indicator that students are moving beyond the literal text and offering an interpretation or critique.

In the transcript that follows, a third-grade class is discussing David Wiesner's picture book *The Three Pigs*. They are talking about various ways the pigs have been illustrated and possible reasons why Wiesner changes the illustration style and color to emphasize the pigs moving in and out of various story worlds.

Ms. H: And then, Katrina said that the dragon pages are black and white, but then . . .

Katrina: They're getting out. They turn color again.

Ms. H: Who is they?

Katrina: The pigs.

Lyle: Back to their own colors.

Serena: Maybe because they're in the dark.

Katrina: And the dragon turns green when the colors are . . .

Ms. H: So Katrina, why do you think that is? Why do you think they're colored here [pointing to the illustrations]?

Katrina: Because they're not in it all the way.

Ms. H: Who's not in it all the way, and what is it?

Lyle: The pigs are not in the page all the way.

Katrina: Because I think they're going to a different book. And, like, the author's pretending a different author made that other book, and so maybe he wanted to make it black and white so that the pigs would go into a different story and turn the same color that the book is supposed to be.

Ms. H: Oh, so the dragon's story is meant to be black and white, so that's why half the pig is black and white and then he's colored because he's coming out of it. Okay, good! What did you notice, Jose?

Jose: Maybe they're different colors because when they are over there in the other story they are like that, and when they go in there they're, like, different colors.

Ms. H: Oh, so maybe when they got into the story they realized they were black and grey and they wanted to . . .

Caleb: Head out!

Ms. H: Head out of the story, so then they became colored again—good! What did you notice besides color? Is there anything besides the color? Is there anything else? Damien, what did you notice about the illustrations?

Damien: Over here on the second page, there's the pig. How did the pig carry all those bricks? I am wondering how can the pig carry all those bricks when it's just the pig and bricks are, like, heavy.

Ms. H: And bricks are really heavy. Okay, so who put the straw on his back?

Although there are numerous possibilities about how to proceed in this discussion, it seems to me that the students were attempting to understand an important aspect of the book, namely that Wiesner portrayed the pigs throughout the story in different colors and different illustrative styles as they moved in and out of the various stories in this postmodern picture book. One student, Katrina, even suggested a plausible reason why this was occurring. She used the word *because* and went on to explain her interpretation about why the pigs changed color and why she believed Wiesner had chosen to create the illustrations in these particular styles. However, rather than expand on this idea, the teacher asked for more comments and eventually ended up wondering how the pig could carry all the bricks. It seems to me that she may have inadvertently overlooked a teachable moment.

Finding the Trigger Points

Many, if not all, of these critical junctures will pass by unnoticed if we are too busy talking to pay attention to them, or if we have not prepared ourselves for the possibilities that may arise by studying the text and illustrations we plan to discuss with our students. In addition, if the pace of our discussions allows for only one voice, teachers will never get the chance to choose which road to travel. We as teachers won't even see the intersection! I have spent considerable time reviewing transcripts like the one offered here, trying to understand the trigger points that enable teachers and students to benefit fully from critical junctures. Here are a few ideas.

1. The teacher in this transcript told me that she didn't really understand the book when she read it herself. That may explain why she let students go in various directions without ever being able to take advantage of their comments. She could have more easily supported the discussion had she been aware of possible themes, topics, or meanings that her students might address. In addition, she would have been in a stronger position had she been prepared to recognize which of her students' comments had "interpretive merit." In other words, she needed to know which comments she could draw upon to expand students' thinking.

2. It is obvious from the transcript that the teacher listened to what the students were saying. However, the primary response she gave students is what I have called "praise and paraphrase." She repeated what was said and offered words like *good*, *Okay*, or *interesting* as her primary response. In other words, she did not take up from, or build on, what had been offered by her students (see Chapter 3).

3. The concept of "interpretive merit" means that we have certain objectives or expectations for a discussion, usually based on our prior readings of the text, that we are hoping to bring forth in our discussions. We certainly want

Interactive Comprehension Strategies: Fostering Meaningful Talk About Text

to hold our expectations tentatively and openly to allow students to make sense of the text in their own way, but we want to notice when students are heading in certain directions. For example, in reading *Tuck Everlasting* by Natalie Babbitt (1975) numerous times with my students, I know that some things will almost certainly arise in our discussions, such as the toad, the concept of life cycles, eternal life, the man in the yellow suit, Winnie Foster's home life, the magic spring, and the music box. I can state that, in most of my discussions, students have addressed some or all of these story elements. If one has not floated to the surface of our discussion, I may just mention it to see what students think. Interpretive merit is a blurred concept, meaning it's hard to describe and define, but we seem to know it when we hear it. It could almost be described as "conditional relevance." Under certain conditions in a discussion, some comments are more relevant than others, and it is our job to determine which paths to go down and which ones to pass by. We can't explore every direction during a discussion, and we need to choose when to slow down and when to get things moving in new directions. On a daily basis, teachers make decisions about which comments to follow and when to politely redirect the discussion. We should base these decisions on which interpretations have more merit—in other words, which interpretations are more viable and offer more possibilities for discussion and rich literary understandings.

4. Ms. H seemed to control the discussion at times to the detriment of the students' engagement. We need to relinquish some control over the discussion—while maintaining order, of course. This is the antithesis of interpretive merit. In other words, we don't want to make every decision about where the discussion is headed or lead students by the nose to predetermined answers. I always ask myself, "What is an important or necessary outcome of reading this particular novel?" This question seems

to have lots of answers, and every teacher may have a different purpose for each novel they read and discuss. I am reluctant to say exactly what a student should get out of a book. I am concerned about students' lived-through experiences as well as what they take away from their readings. In other words, I want students to be engaged with the story, walk in the characters' shoes, think about the events in the story, and construct their own interpretations. What specific ideas students might construct remain open as we proceed.

Closing Comments

Critical junctures are "spaces of possibility," where openings in the discussion allow students freedom to offer their ideas, control the topics of discussion, and move from literal recall of textual elements to interpretation and critique. When students offer inferences that include evidence of interpretive merit, opportunities arise for teachers to capitalize on these teachable moments to develop students' interpretive repertoires. These spaces, while easy to spot when reviewing transcripts of classroom discussions, are more challenging to recognize when we are attending to the on-the-spot discussion. However, we are most successful as teachers when we are aware of our students' textual interpretations and consider the potential they offer for enhancing the thinking of each member of the group. Sometimes we find that taking the road less traveled can make all the difference.

CHAPTER 7

INTERPRETIVE REPERTOIRES

Fostering Students' Comprehension of Text

The goal is not for teachers to abdicate their responsibility for teaching new ideas and clearer ways of expressing them, but to realize that those new ideas will grow best if adults help children make connections between new situations and familiar ones.

—*Courtney Cazden (1986)*

I have come to believe that at the core of our effectiveness as teachers is how we talk and interact with children. The challenge is urging preservice and in-service teachers to attend to their teaching at the level of talk and interaction and make changes that will help expand the way students think and talk about texts. The pressure to cover the curriculum, manage the classroom, assess students' understandings, and follow a prescribed curriculum often overshadows our attention to the way we talk and respond to students. However, it is at the level of talk and interaction that we can make the most significant changes in our instruction and discussions.

In the epigraph by Courtney Cazden, we are reminded that teachers don't abdicate their role in classroom discussions; rather, our role changes from director to knowledgeable facilitator, helping students make sense of their experiences by connecting previous experiences with new ones without limiting what can be thought or how ideas can be expressed. We play an important role in establishing a supportive classroom environment, setting clear and obtainable expectations, helping students make connections across ideas and texts, and articulating their understandings within a community of readers. The goal is not to remove oneself from the discussions, but to gently push students' thinking and expand their interpretive repertoires.

Lecturing to students about our superior interpretations or demanding that they follow the same interpretive path we have chosen to follow through a particular text isn't productive. The *interpretive process* itself is what we want students to experience and consider. As concerned teachers, we often demonstrate how well we read and interpret a text and thus forego opportunities to help students learn how to make sense of what they are reading for themselves. Classroom discussions are not a time for grandstanding or blowing our own intellectual horns; rather, discussions provide a space for supporting students' efforts to understand texts and work through the challenges they encounter. It is in our ability to help students interpret texts, not in our ability to construct sophisticated interpretations in front of them, that the quality of our teaching lies. Unless we unpack our interpretive processes and allow students a view into our thinking, reading will remain for them a closed box.

When students in my university courses tell me that I really made them think during a particular semester, I often wonder what they mean by that statement.

Do they mean that I challenged their beliefs, that I changed their instructional practices, that I confused them, or that I helped them engage in a reflective process and consider their previous knowledge in light of the new concepts, theories, and instructional practices that I shared with them? What I hope it *doesn't* mean is that they have blindly accepted everything I have offered, although at times that might seem easier. Instead, I hope they have considered and reconsidered what we have read and discussed, and that they grew as a result of our experiences together. In other words, I hope I have given them the tools to consider and reconsider the texts they encounter, their theories, and their instructional practices. The best evidence of our teaching is what students do with a text when we are not around!

Implications for Instruction

I think it is best to close out this book with what I consider to be some of the most important implications of the ideas contained herein, and to offer some closing comments on the teaching practices that I envision based on my research and time spent in classrooms. I began this book with the term *preferred vision*, meant to suggest a way that we as teachers might envision the transformation of our classrooms as lively centers of intellectual discussion. Our ability to make significant changes in our instructional practices may well rest on our ability to envision and articulate effective instructional practices. It is to this end that I share these final considerations.

1. Students make more interpretive moves when teachers model the practice. In other words, we learn from the company we keep. If we want students to talk about books in particular ways, we have to show them this preferred way of talking and support their efforts as they move in this direction. If we want students to construct sophisticated interpretations, we need to model more sophisticated interpretations during our discussions and explain our

interpretive processes so students may internalize them as they construct their own.

2. The traditional interaction pattern (IRE) does not support students' thinking. Our discussions should look more like I-R-R-R-R, where an initiating move by the teacher is followed by a series, or chaining, of students' responses. Our discussions should not be back-and-forth ping-pong matches. We need to provide space for our students' voices and ideas.

3. The talk that we promote in our discussions should help students move "beyond the literal" to construct interpretations and analyze the elements, themes, structures, images, and content of a text. While it is important to notice what is contained in the text, the written text and visual images should be viewed not as the primary objective of our discussion but as a *point of departure*.

4. Lively discussions with lots of student interaction are heartening but may not reflect intellectual complexity. Just because students are more involved in our discussions does not necessarily mean they are digging into the text or deepening their interpretive abilities. Certainly, we welcome student talk and engagement, but we also want to keep our ears and eyes on the quality of the conversation—how do our students approach specific topics, and what do they choose to address?

5. We serve as a mediator between our students and the text we are discussing, helping students navigate the text, generate meanings, share their ideas, and consider alternative interpretations. The questions we ask and the perspectives we offer should guide students toward the types of responses we expect them to make on their own.

6. Our responses to students' ideas, comments, and interpretations emphasize what we believe to be important, call attention to what we consider

Interactive Comprehension Strategies: Fostering Meaningful Talk About Text

significant, and signal who is comprehending effectively. We need to attend to how we respond to students' ideas and interpretations so that we don't inadvertently send inappropriate signals. The responses we offer must move beyond "praise and paraphrase" and help extend students' thinking by demonstrating how to articulate, clarify, and confirm their understandings.

7. If we listen hard, we'll discover moments in a discussion when students offer ideas that open up the interactive space for new possibilities. These *critical junctures* are those teachable moments when new ideas are offered for consideration and new directions in the discussion are made possible. When we have familiarized ourselves with the text, prepared ourselves to be effective facilitators of a discussion, and understand how to listen attentively to our students, we are better positioned to take advantage of critical junctures when they occur. We're always deciding which responses to expand and which responses to politely let slip by. It is not an exact science. However, the more we know about our objectives for the lesson, the texts we read, and the needs and abilities of our students, the more often we will recognize the interpretive merit in our students' responses.

8. Finally, it doesn't work to suggest to our students, "I want you to say whatever is on your minds." Although this is certainly an open invitation and may set a warm and welcoming tone for our discussions, it is too open-ended to structure rich and meaningful conversation. The best way to lead our students toward interpretative dialogue is to demonstrate the kinds of discussion we want them to participate in, and show them how to dig deeper into a text during our discussions.

Martin Nystrand (1997) has discussed the importance of *scaffolded talk*. Neil Mercer (2000) talks about *joint intellectual activity* or *inter-thinking*. Aidan Chambers (1996) refers to *shared contemplation*, and I use the term *co-elaboration* to describe interactive book discussions. These terms share much in common, all suggesting classroom talk that invites the sharing of ideas free from teacher domination. They suggest a comingling of ideas and interpretations, an opening up of possibilities in our discussions, a sharing of opinions without fear of ridicule, knowing each voice is welcome, respected, and heard.

Neil Mercer (2000) has suggested that in order to reach a level of joint intellectual activity, groups must have a shared history of ideas and experiences from which to draw; a collective identity where students feel a sense of membership in the community of readers; some reciprocal obligations that provide procedures, rules, and support for interactions; and an "operating discourse," meaning that they have learned and participated in a preferred way of talking. These characteristics are important to consider as we move forward in our professional development.

Still, we can't simply implement the discussion techniques described in Chapter 3 without developing a sense of community and respect among our students. Learning how to make new charts or asking more probing questions will not, on their own, result in more sophisticated discussions. We must care about what our students think, be willing to listen attentively to them, learn effective techniques for facilitating discussions, know enough about the texts we discuss to know how to expand students' interpretive repertoires, and help them generate, articulate, and negotiate more sophisticated interpretations.

In an important analysis of research focusing on classroom discussions, Martin Nystrand (2006) notes that adding as little as one minute of discussion each day can have a significant impact on students' reading abilities. One minute per day! Surely, for the sake of our students' developing intellectual lives, we can invite them to think deeply and give them the time and space to share and explore their ideas. What happens then—beyond the boundaries of one right answer—is often transcendent.

Children's Literature Cited

Avi. (1991). *Nothing but the truth*. New York: Orchard Books.

Babbitt, N. (1975). *Tuck everlasting*. New York: Farrar, Straus & Giroux.

Bloom, B. (1999). *Wolf!* New York: Orchard Books.

Browne, A. (1986). *Piggybook*. New York: Knopf.

Clements, A. (1996). *Frindle*. New York: Aladdin Paperbacks.

Clements, A. (1999). *The Landry News*. New York: Simon & Schuster Books for Young Readers.

Lorbiecki, M. (1998). *Sister Anne's hands*. New York: Dial Books.

Macaulay, D. (1987). *Why the chicken crossed the road*. Boston: Houghton Mifflin.

Macaulay, D. (1990). *Black and white*. New York: Houghton Mifflin.

Martin, B., Jr. (1992). *Brown bear, brown bear, what do you see?* New York: Henry Holt.

Paterson, K. (1977). *Bridge to Terabithia*. New York: HarperTrophy.

Scieszka, J. (1992). *The stinky cheese man and other fairly stupid tales*. New York: Viking.

Sendak, M. (1963). *Where the wild things are*. New York: Harper & Row.

Van Allsburg, C. (1995). *Bad day at Riverbend*. New York: Houghton Mifflin.

Wiesner, D. (2001). *The three pigs*. New York: Clarion Books.

Professional References

Alexander, R. (2006). *Towards dialogic teaching: Rethinking classroom talk* (3rd ed.). Cambridge, UK: Dialogos.

Barnes, D. (1992). *From communication to curriculum* (2nd ed.). Portsmouth, NH: Boynton-Cook.

Britton, J. (1970). *Language and learning*. London: Allen Lane, Penguin Press.

Cazden, C. B. (1986). Classroom discourse. In M. C. Wittrock (Ed.), *Handbook of research on teaching* (pp. 432–463). New York: Macmillan.

Chambers, A. (1996). *Tell me: Children, reading, and talk*. York, ME: Stenhouse.

Dillon, J. T. (1988). *Questioning and teaching*. New York: Teachers College Press.

Goodlad, J. (1984). *A place called school*. New York: McGraw-Hill.

Gutierrez, K., Rymes, B., & Larson, J. (1995). Script, counterscript, and underlife in the classroom: James Brown versus Brown v. Board of Education. *Harvard Educational Review, 65,* 445–471.

Heath, S. B. (1983). *Ways with words: Language, life, and work in communities and classrooms*. New York: Cambridge University Press.

Hoewisch, A. K. (2000). Children's literature in teacher-preparation programs. *Reading Online*. Retrieved June 23, 2008, from http://www.readingonline.org/critical/hoewisch/index.html.

Johnston, P. H. (2004). *Choice words: How our language affects children's learning*. Portland, ME: Stenhouse.

Mercer, N. (1995). *The guided construction of knowledge: Talk amongst teachers and learners.* Clevedon, UK: Multilingual Matters.

Mercer, N. (2000). *Words and minds: How we use language to think together.* London: Routledge.

Myhill, D., Jones, S., & Hopper, R. (2006). *Talking, listening, learning: Effective talk in the primary classroom.* Berkshire, UK: Open University Press.

Nystrand, M. (1997). *Opening dialogue: Understanding the dynamics of language and learning in the English classroom.* New York: Teachers College Press.

Nystrand, M. (2006). Research on the role of classroom discourse as it affects reading comprehension. *Research in the Teaching of English, 40*(4), 392–412.

O'Connor, M. C., & Michaels, S. (1993). Aligning academic task and participation status through revoicing: Analysis of a classroom discourse strategy. *Anthropology and Education Quarterly, 24*(4), 318–335.

Scholes, R. (1985). *Textual power: Literary theory and the teaching of English.* New Haven, CT: Yale University Press.

Serafini, F. (2001). *The reading workshop: Creating space for readers.* Portsmouth, NH: Heinemann.

Serafini, F. (2004). *Lessons in comprehension: Explicit instruction in the reading workshop.* Portsmouth, NH: Heinemann.

Serafini, F., & Giorgis, C. (2003). *Reading aloud and beyond: Fostering the intellectual life with older readers.* Portsmouth, NH: Heinemann.

Serafini, F., & Youngs, S. (2008). *More (advanced) lessons in comprehension: Expanding students' understanding of all types of texts.* Portsmouth, NH: Heinemann.

Sinclair, J. M., & Coulthard, R. M. (1975). *Towards an analysis of discourse: The English used by teachers and pupils.* London: Oxford University Press.

Wells, G. (1989). Language in the classroom: Literacy and collaborative talk. *Language and Education, 3*(4), 251–273.

Index